The Men Who Make Sense of the Destruction

Detective Wil Fuhrman—He walked with a slight stoop, as though bearing the weight of his quarter century investigating the darkest deeds of man. But the phrase *give up* was not a part of his vocabulary. In the toughest arson case in Miami history, he methodically broke down his suspect's cool, cracking the case with razor-sharp interrogation skills.

Captain Bill "Rocky" McAllister—Always optimistic, McAllister was known for the bright grin he wore on his well-chiseled face. But behind the smile, his thirst for justice was unquenchable. He saw arson cases as puzzles—to be solved one piece at a time—and McAllister's methods paid off big in the infamous IWDC warehouse case.

Praise for Charles W. Sasser

Lieutenant James Malvey—"After twenty-five years on the force, I thought I'd seen just about everything." He had . . . until a bearded man bought a dollar's worth of gasoline and set fire to the Happy Land Social Club in the Bronx, igniting the second-largest mass murder in American history.

Lieutenant John Shover—When the Alaskan fishing boat *Investor* was burned to the gunnels, the only clues left were the cremated remains of an unknown number of people. By force of sheer willpower, Lieutenant Shover took charge and threw out the rule books in "the biggest one-time crime in Alaskan history."

Praise for Charles W. Sasser's

One Shot—One Kill

Detective Bruce Duncan—When two corpses were found burned to a crisp in a car trunk in Sapulpa, Oklahoma, Detective Duncan showed the mettle of a true arson investigator. Following a dizzying array of clues, he protected the local residents from the ultimate threat—a serial criminal turned arsonist.

John Cabaniss—During nearly 40 years' tenure as a justice of the peace, Cabaniss had become immune to any fear of death. "I can go see a body in a field that is rising and falling with maggots and still eat rice for supper," he is fond of saying. So he was more than prepared to deal with the carnage at the Waco massacre—or so he thought. . . .

Praise for Charles W. Sasser's
Homicide!

Other Books by Charles W. Sasser

Doc: Platoon Medic (coauthored with Daniel E. Evans Jr.)
Smoke Jumpers
Always a Warrior
Homicide!
Last American Heroes (coauthored with Michael Sasser)
The 100 Kill
One Shot—One Kill (coauthored with Craig Roberts)
Shoot to Kill
The Walking Dead (coauthored with Craig Roberts)
First SEAL (coauthored with Roy Boehm)

Available from POCKET BOOKS

FIRE COPS

Michael Sasser and Charles W. Sasser

POCKET BOOKS
New York   London   Toronto   Sydney   Tokyo   Singapore

An *Original* Publication of POCKET BOOKS

POCKET BOOKS, a division of Simon & Schuster Inc.
1230 Avenue of the Americas, New York, NY 10020

ISBN: 978-1-4767-8445-8

First Pocket Books printing February 1998

10 9 8 7 6 5 4 3 2 1

POCKET and colophon are registered trademarks of Simon & Schuster Inc.

Front cover photo © Tomas Muscionico, 1991/PNI

Printed in the U.S.A.

This book is dedicated to
the fire cops themselves.

Authors' Note

The information in this book was derived from a variety of sources—extensive personal interviews, official reports from law-enforcement agencies, media accounts. Re-created events and dialogue are witnesses' and participants' best recollections of what was said and done. Quite naturally, one person's interpretation of events will never be exactly the same as another's.

In addition, we have filtered this information, selecting, emphasizing, and discarding. Any errors that may inadvertently occur through this complicated process are regretted and unintentional.

Names of firefighters, arson investigators, other law-enforcement officers, and convicted suspects still incarcerated are the real names of actual persons. As a rule, we have changed the names of witnesses, most crime victims, juvenile offenders, suspects released back into society, and other people somehow involved in these events for whom public exposure would serve no good purpose.

AUTHORS' NOTE

For the sake of clarity, events have sometimes been condensed, telescoped, or transposed in order to fit into the story line, without sacrificing veracity or accuracy.

Finally, we wish to thank the people who made this book possible—the nation's fire cops, named or unnamed in this account. Their help in the monumental task of researching and writing this book made a difficult project an enjoyable experience.

—Michael Sasser and Charles W. Sasser

FIRE
COPS

Introduction

Arsonists are literally burning up America. *Webster's New World Dictionary* defines *arson* as "the crime of purposely setting fire to a building or property. . . ." The National Fire Protection Association reports that 100,000 fires annually are of an incendiary or suspicious nature, roughly 14% of all fires. Each year, they kill 700 to 800 people, injure 3,500, and cause an estimated $2 *billion* in damage losses. Total insurance fraud is estimated to run up an annual tab of $16 *billion* to $20 *billion.* Yet arson is the most underreported and unsolved crime of all the Federal Bureau of Investigation (FBI) index crimes.

Fire was one of man's first tools—and remains one of his oldest enemies. Today, it is often the weapon of choice for swindlers and murderers, carrying as it does a pitiful arrest and conviction rate. As a typical example, there were approximately 95,000 arsons in 1989, resulting in only 15,000 arrests—a successful closure rate of about 15%. Unlike murderers, kidnappers, and robbers, the majority of arsonists remain undiscovered and unindicted.

In most criminal actions, it is easy to prove at least

that a crime has been committed: the dead body lies there for the police to see; a burglar leaves a broken window behind and takes with him his victim's TV and VCR. Arson leaves no such obvious clues: any evidence of arson is very often consumed by the fire itself; plus, many fire starters are amateurs without criminal records. That makes tracking and convicting them even more challenging.

FBI statistics published in the Uniform Crime Report note that 40% of all suspects *arrested* for arson are juveniles under 18 years of age. Thirty percent of these juveniles are under age 15; 7% are under age 10. Arson may accompany a range of other crimes or may be the first step to a life of crime. Half of all juvenile suspects have been in trouble with authorities before, for offenses ranging from petty stealing to manslaughter. Research reveals that an abnormally high number of serial killers begin their careers by torturing pets and starting fires. David "Son of Sam" Berkowitz and Ted Bundy, among others, were early fire starters.

Eleventh-century England looked upon arson with such dread that arsonists were sentenced to death when apprehended. At the time of Henry II (A.D. 1154–1189), arsonists were banished from the kingdom or punished by having a hand or foot cut off. In the United States, first-degree arson—the torching of any dwelling or attached building—carries a penalty of up to 20 years in prison. It is murder if anyone dies as a result of arson.

In 1979, by congressional mandate, arson was added to the U.S. Justice Department's Uniform Crime Report, Part I Crime Index, which includes the violent crimes of murder, nonnegligent homicide, forcible rape, robbery, and aggravated assault and the property crimes of burglary, larceny, and auto theft. Previously, arson had not been considered a major crime and had been catalogued as a Part II crime, along with drunken driving, gambling, and other such offenses.

FIRE COPS

Fires are started for revenge, for profit, for excitement, for recognition, out of fear, and to cover other crimes. Arsonists include grandmothers who are arson ring leaders, jilted lovers, Mafia members, teens seeking revenge against schoolteachers, teenage dope dealers, respected lawyers, businesspeople, and volunteer firefighters.

Motives, fire investigators find, generally fall into one of five broad categories, the most prevalent of which is simple vandalism. Vandalism—usually by children and teens—accounts for about 40% of all arsons, usually of the nuisance variety, such as trash cans or abandoned buildings set afire. David "Son of Sam" Berkowitz confessed to setting more than 2,000 such fires in the Brooklyn–Queens area before he moved up to shooting courting couples at night. Fire starting fits in with the other two elements of the "homicidal triad": bed-wetting and cruelty to animals.

The second most prevalent motive is the profit motive. During an economic recession, the owners of businesses and stores sometimes resort to using fire as a way to get out from underneath mortgages or to escape their losses by collecting insurance. Veteran fire investigators refer to the "accidental" loss to fire of a failing business or decaying structure as "urban renewal."

Businesspeople may eliminate competition by torching a rival's business. Disgruntled partners may burn out their firm to recoup an investment. In some instances, professional fire starters advertise their services by word of mouth, gaining reputations and some wealth in their abilities to make fires appear entirely God's will. One New York City landlord paid to have 26 of his own buildings burned down for the insurance money. In a few instances, carpenters and insurance agents have been known to go around setting fires in order to generate new business. Some enterprising entrepreneurs develop elaborate schemes to start busi-

3

nesses with the ultimate intent to collect fire insurance on their predictable losses.

The third motive category is revenge. After a nasty divorce, an ex-husband sneaks up one night to his former residence and burns down the house with his ex-wife in it. A man burns down a fast-food restaurant because the chain refuses to settle over a fish bone he claims had gotten stuck in his throat. A fired employee gets even by striking a match to his boss's office. In New York, four men are indicted for crashing a car into the lobby of an apartment house and setting it afire in retaliation against residents who complained to police about their drug dealing. In Los Angeles, a man who lost $50 on a rock cocaine deal is arrested for setting a fire that kills a handicapped woman. Still other revenge motives involve labor disputes, have racial overtones, or are the result of terrorism or mob action.

New York City Fire Marshal James McSwigin describes a typical revenge arsonist as a man angry at his girlfriend for seeing—sometimes just for talking to—another man.

"This type of fire setter is probably one of the most dangerous because he's usually enraged when he's starting the fire. But he's usually the easiest to catch. In his rage, he'll try to burn her out, or burn the new boyfriend, with a Molotov cocktail or by squeezing flammable liquid under the door and he won't care who sees him or about anything else. Consequently, his crime of arson isn't surreptitious."

To many arson investigators, the most perplexing of the fire starter motives, the most difficult to comprehend psychologically, is the fourth category, which falls under the broad heading of *pyromania*, which literally means "fire madness" and refers to people who are driven to start fire in the same way that alcoholics are driven to drink and drug addicts are driven to take dope. The true pyromaniac possesses no rational motive for starting fires, other than delusions that center around flame as a sexual or adrenaline stimulant.

Such people generally live unhappy lives. Most are males, the adults living alone in shabby surroundings and having little social life. Typically, pyromaniacs use public portions of buildings to start fires, favorite sites being hallways and cellars. They almost always use matches with rags, papers, or trash to start their fires. The need to watch the fire after they set it often leads to detection, particularly when the pyro plays the role of the helpful hero. Often they stand among onlookers at a fire, hands in pockets, masturbating.

One woman turned in her boyfriend to authorities because he kept reeking of smoke when he showed up to seek sex. It turned out that the only time he *could* have sex was after he set a fire.

The clearest evocation of the obscure linkage between sex and watching things burn comes from the confessions of a German arsonist, Peter Kurten.

"During the firing of the haystacks," he said, "the thought that human beings might be burned added to the sensations that I experienced. The shouting of the people and the glare of the fire pleased me. During big fires, I always had an orgasm.

"If you see in my confession sometimes several arsons in one night, then I had no success with the first or second. I also had an orgasm when I fired the woods. It was a lovely sight when one pine after the other was consumed in the flames fanned by a sharp east wind. That was wonderful!"

The first place to look for a suspect, say veteran arson investigators, is in the crowd watching the blaze.

In the fifth motive category, criminals have been known to use fire to attempt to cover up other crimes, such as murder, embezzlement, or burglary. The problem with this motive, as most criminals discover to their dismay, is that rather than cover up the deed, fire may actually bring attention to the original crime.

Next to war, arson is humanity's costliest act of violence. The incendiary time bomb in the United States ticks off one arson fire every 5 minutes. Against this ticking bomb and the criminals who would employ it against society stands a thin line of investigators, part firefighter, part cop, with the authority to arrest: *fire cops.*

Chapter

1

Miami, Florida

At night, viewed from the sky, cities jammed onto the beaches of south Florida resemble strings of flickering jewels delineating the shape of the peninsula. Fort Lauderdale, Hallendale, Pompano Beach, Coral Gables, Miami—glimmering necklaces and brooches on the black cloth bosom of a rich fat lady. Stones are missing here and there where there are warehouses and industrial areas with either few lights or lights extinguished after normal business hours.

In one of those dark areas at the west end of Miami International Airport, just beyond six-lane Palmetto Expressway, passengers taking off on September 3 aboard an American Airlines 4 A.M. red-eye bound for Houston, Dallas, and beyond spotted a bright explosion, like a flashbulb going off in a darkened stadium. A grandmother on her way to visit a sister in Phoenix thought another airliner had crashed. Excited, she summoned a flight attendant.

"There!" she exclaimed, pointing. "In the dark at the end of the airport."

The detonation swelled, then diminished to a fire

glow distinguishable from other city lights only by its isolation.

"It's not a plane crash," the flight attendant assured passengers. "It's probably a fire. There are a bunch of warehouses on the west end of the runway."

"I don't see any fire engine lights," protested the apprehensive grandmother.

The attendant laughed. She was a Miami native. "We'll be flying over Tampa before the fire department gets there," she said.

Station 16, Metro–Dade Fire Department, had had an earlier alarm to a blaze on Tamiami Trail. It turned out to be a trash-can fire, a garbage run. Firefighters had just stripped again and crawled into their second-story bunks when the alarms tossed them back onto the floor.

"Warehouse," intoned the radio dispatcher through the in-station intercom. "International Warehouse Distributing Corporation, IWDC, Northwest 14th Street and 79th Avenue."

Then followed a long list of assignments: "Engine one, engine three, ladder one, rescue two . . ."

They were emptying the firehouse.

"It's a blitzkrieg!" somebody shouted, hopping on one foot to get into his heavy boots and turnouts, then taking the stairs in a headlong rush. "The entire warehouse district must be going up!"

Chief Ed Neafsey, commander of Fire Battalion 7, was a crusty veteran. He sniffed the smoke-filled air from blocks away as he sirened his command vehicle to the scene. The smell was of wood smoke—strong, as if a lumberyard might be burning. However, it was more acrid, bitter—the taste and smell of raw bile after a bad night in a bad bar.

A bleeping, lights-flashing entourage of engines and ladder trucks streamed into the maze of night-dark warehouses. The entire area was block after block of low-spread concrete block structures, identical in beige and brown except for their varying sizes. A gigantic plume of black smoke, twisting like a captured tornado, its undersides glowing red, tethered itself to the flat roof of the IWDC building, setting it apart from all the others.

The IWDC, at 7952 N.W. 14th Street, covered an area slightly larger than a football field. Other warehouses backed up to within 15 feet of it, while the docking doors and offices on the other side opened into a wide parking lot. The sound inside the warehouse as fire equipment surrounded it was that of a 747 jet trying to take off—the roaring of a trapped fire monster. It had already burst through the flat tar roof in several places. Flames blew out the cracks, slapping and snapping at the darkened sky.

Firefighters in their SCBAs—self-contained breathing apparatus, like its underwater cousin, SCUBA gear, with air tanks and hoses and masks—resembled a bunch of baggy Darth Vaders as they began laying pipe and dogging ladders. The entire building was already at risk. The fire had either been burning inside a long time, smoldering, until it ate through and infused and invigorated itself with fresh oxygen, causing a blow-up—or the building had actually caught fire with the explosion seen from the American Airlines plane flying over.

Firefighters would face another San Francisco–type fire if flames skipped to the building next door and kept going, eating from structure to structure in a conflagration that might literally consume the dozen or so square blocks of the warehouse district. Fortunately, there were no residences nearby.

Air vents, crawl spaces, and heating and air-conditioning ducts inside the building served as chimneys and travel routes for self-propagating flames. Well ventilated, fueled by whatever goods the warehouse held, the fire raced past office windows and around doors, licking out through the roof and hurling ashes at its neighbors. It created its own wind, sucking in surrounding oxygen with the velocity of a small gale. Papers and other debris skittered across the docking yards, being sucked into the inferno.

A fire command officer could be compared to a general commanding troops in battle, planning strategy and tactics, weakening the enemy here with heavy artillery, withdrawing there to a defensive perimeter, probing or scouting or attacking into enemy territory, finally, perhaps, launching an all-out offensive to defeat and drive the enemy into submission.

Chief Neafsey ordered a two-front attack, from the street side and the parking–docking area, with squads covering rear and left exposures to contain the blaze and prevent its spread. Truckies launched a separate assault from the air with their long hydraulic ladders and heavy water cannon. Other firefighters patrolled the vicinity with booster lines to contain flying embers. It was a surround and drown, purely a defensive tactic. The fire was out of control, preventing a direct interior attack.

The IWDC warehouse burned for a total of 14 hours. It was a four-alarmer. More than 135 firefighters took part in the predawn battle, along with 30 fire engines and ladder, aerial, and fire rescue vehicles. The bitter smoke was saturated with poisonous chemical fumes. Twenty-five fighters were injured from smoke inhalation, contact dermatitis, chest pains. Local emergency departments treated some of them for painful skin blisters.

The building had to cool for at least 24 hours before fire investigators, along with representatives of the Environmental Protective Agency (EPA) and Haz-Mat—Hazardous Materials—dared enter it. At dawn on September 3, the building sat steaming in a veritable lake of filthy blackish water. Several million gallons of water had been used to douse the flames. Some firefighter with a nautical sense of humor put a sign on his fire truck that read: 12 mph. No-Wake Zone.

The contents of the building appeared to be a complete loss, charred beyond easy recognition. Useless debris remained beneath collapsed roof and walls in toxic rubble 10 feet high and all but impossible to penetrate. Metal doors were heat-warped and twisted, while great blackened-lip holes pockmarked the roof where either flames had chewed through or firefighters had ventilated.

Nearby, two fire cops who had been summoned from bed in the middle of the night fortified themselves with black coffee and eggs at an all-night eatery off the Palmetto Expressway while they waited for the warehouse to cool. Dade County, Florida, which includes Miami, dispatched arson investigators—fire cops—to the scene of every major fire that appeared the least suspect. Big blazes in warehouses and storage areas were always suspicious.

Wil Fuhrman was a Metro–Dade police detective assigned to the arson squad. Middle-aged, he walked slightly stooped, as if bearing the weight of the police cynicism collected from his quarter century of investigating the foibles and crimes of mankind. Deliberate and methodical, he sometimes looked as burned out as the charred shells of the buildings into whose black bowels he trudged to ply his trade.

He often worked with his breakfast partner, Captain Bill "Rocky" McAllister, head of the Metro–Dade Fire Department's arson investigation squad. McAllister was short and stocky and had a handsome, well-chiseled face and thin brown hair matted to his head by the uniform ball cap he wore. Whereas Fuhrman was well into middle age, McAllister was only entering that zone. He always greeted life, even at this early hour, with a bright grin. Fuhrman sometimes grumbled that McAllister liked his job so well he would work if the county cut his wages by half.

"Got you out of bed too?" McAllister had said when the two men met at the warehouse fire.

"McAllister, it's 5 A.M., for Christ's sake. Where else would I be?"

"You got out on the wrong side too."

"What?"

"Wrong side of the bed."

"McAllister, is there a *right* side to the bed this early in the morning?"

The *real* investigation began after the fire was extinguished and the building was cool enough to allow the fire cops to venture inside with their shovels. The shovel is still the fire investigator's most essential tool. No matter how far the profession's technology might advance, the fire cop still starts a probe with the shovel and spends the first hours—even days—of investigation digging around in ashes, seeking clues and answers.

In the meantime, the sad-faced cop and the grinning fire investigator observed the fire for clues as to fuel and point of origin, acquiring what knowledge they could from observations. Fighters in the heat of battle could not be expected to worry about preserving evidence. They chopped holes in roofs for ventilation, kicked out windows, tore down walls, and soaked everything with thousands of gallons of water. After all that, a fire cop had to be exceptionally skillful to come up with anything useful. The problem with working arson as a crime, unlike homicide, for example, was that the "smoking gun," the scene's best evidence, often went up in smoke.

It sometimes annoyed McAllister how two masked men could hold up a Miami Savings & Loan for $25,000 and make front pages all over the nation, whereas some case in which a guy torched a business in a $10 *million* insurance fraud scam barely made a local 1-inch column on page F-42.

Observations at the fire scene turned up at least three important facts. First, almost the entire warehouse was totally involved in flames; few *unintentional* fires involved an entire structure all at once. Second, the chemical taste and smell of the smoke was overcoming firefighters. Third, the fire started with an explosion, another unusual occurrence. A metal pedestrian door at the end of the warehouse nearest the street had been blown off its hinges and halfway across the parking lot. Near where it came to rest, McAllister picked up a molten wad of what had once been a hand-held AM/FM portable two-way radio—a walkie-talkie. The brand name was still readable: Realistic.

Radios could be used either as detonating devices or for communications between the fire starter and his lookout.

"Maybe the fire starter got caught inside when he lit her up," McAllister suggested.

"That's poetic," Fuhrman growled. "No such luck. How about breakfast? They're going to be dumping water on this thing for hours."

Over their breakfast table, Rocky sipped black hot coffee while his partner held up a fist and lifted one finger at a time to tick off his suspicions.

"Point one: total involvement," Fuhrman said. "Point two: explosion as from an accelerant. Three: it occurred at 4 A.M. when there would be no witnesses. Four: warehouses are always prime targets for fire insurance fraud. Point five: that warehouse burned quick and *smelled* like it was full of something flammable." He set down his coffee cup so he could use his other hand. "Six: do you want to bet that building and its contents carry an insurance policy heavy enough to choke a race horse at Hialeah?"

"You've convinced me," McAllister conceded. "It's likely arson."

The waitress, in a checkered half apron and a hair net, freshened their coffee and took their orders. She wanted to talk about the fire.

"One of our regulars came in and said it looked like everything over there was burning," she said. "We heard the sirens. You can see the smoke from out back. How'd it start?"

"Probably not from somebody smoking in bed," McAllister joked.

She laughed. "I'm *so* afraid of fire. I used to have these nightmares about getting burnt up while I was sleeping. I couldn't wake up enough to get away. You know how it is when you're dreaming. Like you can't move or you move in *real* slow motion."

Fuhrman interrupted, impatient. "Eggs?"

"Over easy, right? Is it really like that when you get burnt up—like you can't move or something when you know the fire's coming?"

She cast a glance at Fuhrman. "Eggs coming up," she chirped and bustled off, hips swinging.

"Don't burn them," McAllister chided her.

When she returned with two egg platters balanced in her hands and her curiosity intact, she asked, "Anybody burnt up in the fire over there?"

"We don't know yet," McAllister responded. Fuhrman started eating.

"I heard things," the waitress continued in a hushed voice, bending near. "What's it look like when people get burnt up?"

Chapter

2

Carroll County, Virginia

Fire investigators all knew the answer to that question—what it looked like to be burned. It was the smell of the corpses, sweetish, sickly, like spoiled steak on charcoals, and it was the grisly sight of bodies blackened, appendages burned off, muscles contracted by the heat until the remains knotted into final fetal positions.

On December 5, Carroll County Sheriff's Captain Rick Clark Jr., a certified fire investigator, attended an autopsy at Roanoke Community Hospital for 30-year-old Sheila Marie Ring and her 2-year-old daughter Jasmine Sutphin. The pathologist wheeled in the bodies one at a time on a little gurney and transferred them to a stainless-steel table with drainage capacity for the body fluids. Both corpses bore the char and deep redness of second- and third-degree burns. The little girl's blackened hands were frozen into place, splayed in front of her face as though to protect it from attack or approaching flames.

The pathologist went to work with little saws and scalpels and knives, removing the skullcap to expose the brain for examination, prying open the carcass from sternum to pubic bone as if gutting a slain deer. The first time Clark saw an autopsy, he had had to escape outside for fresh air to avoid being sick. Now, he steeled himself for what had to be done. It was part of his job as an investigator, a job that by this point he'd held for 2 decades, a long time removed from the vulnerability of his rookie days.

"Where were they, exactly, when you found the bodies?" the pathologist asked.

Dark-haired, pretty Sheila Ring and her tiny blond daughter Jasmine had, until the fateful night of December 3, lived in a small three-bedroom house in the lovely Buckwood section off State Route 735 in the rural heart of Virginia's Blue Ridge Mountains. Two raccoon hunters working their hounds in the tall timber hollow behind the residence spotted the glow of fire—a big fire—through the winter-denuded hardwood forest. They ran to the nearest farmhouse and rang the Hillsville Volunteer Fire Department.

"That pretty divorcée's place—Sheila's—it's burning hard!"

The house was totally involved by the time seven volunteer firefighters swerved two pumpers into the yard. The nearest neighbor from down the road had cut across the field and was trying to find a garden hose; he was also Sheila's landlord, from whom she had rented the house for the past two years. He pointed at a blue Mustang parked so near the house that the heat was starting to curl the paint and blacken the windows.

"That's Sheila's car! I think she and the baby are still in there!"

Water sloshed onto the ground began to freeze—it was that cold in the mountain air. Firefighters made several attempts to enter the inferno before attacking hose crews beat back flames enough to permit two of their number to crawl into the house. Using flashlights, the two volunteers worked their way through dense smoke to a back bedroom.

FIRE COPS

That was where they found Sheila——or at least the charred remains of her body. The smoky beams from flashlights traveled along a heat-bloated body completely nude except for a bra. She lay on the floor in a partly reclined position against the smoldering bed.

Next to her lay the child clad only in a long T-shirt.

Both bodies were dragged outside and deposited on the winter-brown lawn, where the neighbor landlord took one sickened look at them and proclaimed them to be Sheila and her baby daughter.

"It looks like they were trapped back there and couldn't get out," said one of the firefighters. "God almighty!"

Carroll County Sheriff Dick Carrico and his fire investigator, Captain Clark, were back at the fire site at first light. All that remained standing of the house were the walls, and sections of them had collapsed. The recovered bodies had been sent to Roanoke for autopsy, which Clark would witness later in the day. The two big men sifted their way through the ruins.

A wood-burning stove crouched in the living-room ashes, looking somehow sullen and guilty. Clark knelt and studied the extent of the damage near the stove, at first expecting to find that an ember blown or escaped from the stove might have started the fire. Wood-burning stoves were always suspect.

After studying burn patterns for a few minutes, the fire cop duck-walked across the living room and stopped some 10 feet in front of the stove. He scrutinized his surroundings for several minutes while Sheriff Carrico watched. He felt the ashes, noted their color and distribution. Coning, the way a fire starts from a particular point and then spreads in a fan- or conelike pattern, revealed the fire had started here, *away* from the stove, and that it had burned *here* first and hottest.

"The fire," he said at last, "started over here."

"There? Could an ember have jumped that far from the stove?"

Clark stood up and faced the uniformed lawman. Many rural sheriffs wore either jeans and cowboy boots or business suits. Carrico preferred a uniform.

Clark said, "This fire was no accident. It was *set.*"

Outside, near an outbuilding, lay the stiffened dead body of Sheila's breedless mutt of a dog. Upon closer examination, the lawmen discovered its throat had been slit down to the bone.

Chapter

3

Investigating arson—particularly arson resulting in homicide—takes patience and time. Open-and-shut cases in which a crime is committed at 8 P.M. and the perpetrator is in jail by midnight are a rarity, except for "crimes of passion" in which hormones and hot blood incite rash behavior. Some guy is pissed at his girl-friend, douses her with gasoline, and whips out his Bic. Or some battered wife finally gets fed up and sheets her drunken loafer of a husband to the bed and torches his two-timing ass.

Patience and attention to detail must be acquired. The investigator must prove arson *before* proving hom-icide, if a death was involved, and arson is undoubtedly the crime for which it is the most difficult of all to establish *corpus delicti*—the so-called body of the crime. Fuel loads, venting and oxygen feeds, point of fire origin, building contents, sprinkler and electrical systems, owners, insurers . . . all play a role in the investigation. Good fire investigators learn to control their initial eagerness and to methodically follow the crime trail one painstaking step at a time.

In Miami, Fire Captain Rocky McAllister still remembered how surprised he had been when he put on his first fire hat. The steel-lined head gear was no mere hat. It was a protective machine of reinforced battering-ram material, bristling with the bolt shafts and nuts that held it together. The cracked shield on the front was emblazoned with METRO–DADE FIRE DEPT. The regal brass topknot had been bashed in by what must have been a stunning blow to the head of its former wearer.

Combating fires was a one-shift-at-a-time affair. You answered the alarm and fought the blaze to a standstill; then that particular event was all over. History. It required some adjusting for McAllister when he switched from fighting fires to investigating them, as his interest now focused not so much on extinguishing fires as it did on *why* fires started and *who*, in the case of arson, did the starting. Instead of fighting a fire and forgetting about it the same day, arson investigators frequently work on cases that drag on for days, weeks, months.

"You observe me and you'll catch on to how it's done," an old-time fire cop advised McAllister when he first transferred out of station houses to fire investigations.

They drove to a bar on Biscayne Boulevard that a bar patron had threatened to burn down and then apparently attempted to carry out his threat. McAllister's trainer invited witnesses into his car one at a time, where he questioned them. McAllister sat in the backseat, interrupting with particularly insightful questions in his eagerness to get down to the main point.

Finally, the trainer calmly asked the current witness if he would mind stepping out of the car for a moment. As soon as the guy closed the door, the trainer turned on McAllister.

"This is not a fucking fire you're trying to put out," he growled. "You open your mouth one more time when I'm talking and I'm going to jam my notebook down your throat. These things take time. I'll give you as much time to ask questions as you want—when I'm finished. Is that clear?"

It was a valuable lesson in patience that all fire cops have to learn, especially those who were first firefighters.

Chapter

4

Miami, Florida

Bill Hamilton was a lean, patient man of average height, athletic, with a face as sharp as a hatchet blade topped by short-cropped brown hair. A Vietnam combat veteran with the Marines, he was in his forties. He stood knee-deep in a pile of charred rubble that the preceeding week had been the Okeelanta Sugar Refinery in Florida's far-western Palm Beach County.

He pried loose a file cabinet baked to black ash and instantly rusted from heat oxidation. Nearby, his partner, Jerry Hopkins, pulled out a twist of electrical conduit and sorted through the ashes and debris of what might have been an office desk. They worked with their ever-trusty shovels in what remained of the three-story, two-block-long section of warehouse used primarily by the sugar refinery to store tools, machinery, and spare equipment. The huge processing building and a storage building containing 25,000 tons of raw sugar—along with rats the size of cats—had survived the fire.

Nearby, crane operators lifted twisted I-beams and slabs of debris from the burn. One crane was hooked to a slab of roofing that must first be freed by a cutting torch. From the rubble of concrete, half-melted machinery, scorched soda machines, and burned-out file cabinets, other investigators carried out several fuel cans, some of them with tops removed. Others sorted through electrical conduits and dug around for pipes and wiring belonging to heaters or air conditioners.

What they looked for, going through the layers, digging down to the origin of the fire, were signs of arson, something out of place, something that didn't belong. Like empty gas cans, electrical boxes shorted out, residue from an accelerant. Gasoline and other fuels often seeped into wood or cracks and did not always disappear with the flames.

While some professional arsonists know so much about fuel loads, venting, and oxygen feeds that they can take down a building in the middle of a block without damaging the structures on either side, others make serious mistakes. Hamilton had worked on one case in which a fire starter poured a "trailer" of gasoline from upstairs in an apartment down the stairway to the front door. Gasoline fumes were so thick that by the time he struck his match, the resulting vapor explosion fried him in his shoes. It took investigators 3 days to find his charred body and solve the case.

Hamilton and Hopkins, stationed out of Miami, were the FBI of arson investigators——federal agents from the Bureau of Alcohol, Tobacco and Firearms (BATF) assigned as members of national response teams to investigate and to assist local authorities in investigating arsons of high property and monetary losses and arsons in which life is lost.

In the United States, 30% to 40% of all *intentionally* set fires go unrecognized, primarily because of the lack of qualified fire investigators. Although most large cities, such as Miami, Detroit, and Los Angeles, employ fire marshals or specially trained investigators as members of either the fire departments or the police departments, such as in Dade County, Florida, with Captain Rocky McAllister of the fire department and Detective Wil Fuhrman of the police department, many smaller municipalities and rural areas either ignore the issue altogether or use part-time or untrained detectives in their fire investigations. In Carroll County, Virginia, for example, Sheriff's Deputy Rick Clark, investigating the mysterious fire deaths of Sheila Ring and her 2-year-old daughter, Jasmine, was primarily a law-enforcement officer and investigator crosstrained to recognize some of the indications and clues of criminal fire starting.

In recent decades, arson for profit has turned into a national nightmare. In 1972, Washington established the BATF to replace "revenuers" in keeping tabs on the production and distribution of liquor and tobacco products and in regulating firearms and explosives. It didn't take much stretching of the rules to place Molotov cocktails and other incendiary devices in the category of explosives, thus expanding BATF duties to include arson investigations. Bill Hamilton was among the first agents trained in arson investigations.

In 1980, BATF created four National Response Teams, each stationed in a quadrant of the United States to tackle arson, from prevention to prosecution, and to coordinate efforts among local, state, and federal governments. It assembled the most qualified people and the finest equipment available, including 29 response trucks that could be driven to a scene or loaded aboard U.S. Coast Guard airplanes and flown to a site. Each team included agents trained in investigating arson and bombings, forensic chemistry, cause and origin detection, and explosives technology. War had finally been declared on big-time professional torches and a free-for-all industry of insurance-defrauding fire starters.

Of particular importance in the investigation of major arson cases were the creation of the BATF arson forensics laboratory in Atlanta, Georgia, and the training of specialists in arson auditing and arson profiling.

The bureau's laboratory pioneered many of the techniques used in forensic labs to detect accelerants and the use of scraps of clothing, charred wood, and other materials to reconstruct crime scenes. Chemists could isolate gasoline samples to their specific manufacturers. Specialists compared microscopic threads, wire, and other evidence to samples of similar material recovered from a suspect's car or home. Fingerprint powders and dust went out history's back window as crime-scene search specialists turned to lasers to search for fingerprints on glass fragments, partially melted containers, and heated doorknobs.

Professional auditors fought racketeering and organized crime by following "paper trails" inch by inch, piece by piece through the corporate records of a suspect business to determine who profited most from a fire and if other crimes might be planned or concealed.

BATF patterns its own behavioral science unit after that of the FBI, which became famous for its profiling of serial killers. Arson profiling uses the same process of analyzing crime scene evidence and modus operandi to form personality profiles of offenders, thus enabling investigators to use computers to track suspects through related crimes and to actually predict or isolate at least the *type* of fire starter involved in a particular fire.

In overcoming initial local resentment to the federal government's intrusion, Hamilton and other federal experts argued convincingly that "you can look at the aftermath of a big fire and understand that locally you don't have the manpower to work it. BATF can bring in ten or twenty people on a team and another six or seven local BATF people with experience and conduct an investigation that would take your local departments months to do."

Arson investigation had gone high tech. Yet, much of the fire cop's work—most of it, in fact—still involved a shovel and scrounging around in ashes.

Hamilton compared his job to that of a pathologist—only instead of conducting autopsies on human cadavers, he conducted them on corpses of steel and wood and concrete. The sugar refinery died of fire, no doubt of that, but did someone pour the gas and light the match or set the timer? Or was it an accidental death caused by a faulty electrical outlet or a discarded cigarette butt?

A dozen years and a thousand burn sites had taught the fire cop to look at the aftermath of a blaze and re-create in his mind the way flames work, to follow them back down the roof, along the hallways, and around corners and into other rooms, sucking the fire back to one spot, like a movie running in reverse.

When Belle Glade firefighters arrived at the refinery fire shortly after 5 A.M., a huge blaze burned in the warehouse high in one corner, close to the ceiling, lighting up the predawn sky. They assumed the fire originated there near the roof, although it seemed to violate one of the rules of a natural fire—that flames do not travel from a high source to a lower point without some kind of help.

Hamilton and Hopkins worked their way through the debris from the least-damaged areas of the refinery to the most severely burned. A covered conveyance belt ran along below the roof line from the processing section to the attached storage warehouse. The presumed origin of the fire was high on the north side of the structure near the conveyance belt. However, it puzzled Hamilton that the wooden floor beneath this area remained largely intact, while the floor at the southeast corner was nothing but ash. A metal storage cabinet crumbled in Hamilton's hands.

"The greatest heat was *here*," he said, theorizing. He pointed. "Gases and smoke created by the burn traveled along the covered conveyor belt, like through the flue of a potbellied stove, looking to escape in the taller warehouse building. They collected in the upper ceiling and couldn't vent fast enough. The fumes reignited. Firefighters couldn't see anything but smoke, so they assumed the fire was burning fuel, not vapors."

The fire, he concluded, started low in the southeast corner, not high in the roof on the north.

Although the BATF National Response Teams can determine the causes of nine of 10 fires they investigate, some fire causes simply can't be pinpointed without a reasonable doubt. Arson investigation, for all its being high tech, is not a true science. Bill Hamilton rocked back in his chair in his Miami office, on the phone with Captain Rocky McAllister, head of the Metro–Dade Fire Department's arson squad. Regretfully, Hamilton had listed the cause of the sugar refinery fire as "undetermined." He hoped this newest case—the previous night's fire at the IWDC warehouse that had resulted in an estimated $12 *million* in damage—could be concluded more successfully.

"Get your thoroughbreds together," McAllister said with a chuckle. "Everything about this says it was torched by a professional. Firefighters are still doing overhaul this morning. It can stay hot in there for days."

Miami headquarters for BATF was lodged in a modern office building complex five blocks west of the Palmetto Expressway off Northwest 20th Street. A small sign in the lobby listed the bureau as occupying an entire suite on the fourth floor. Hamilton's cubbyhole office was studded with the accoutrements and mementos of his trade—fire hat, boots, turnout gear, nozzles, a fire ax—and littered with papers, maps, graphs, news clippings, and other clutter. The most visible object in the room was a well-used shovel leaning against the wall next to the door. For all the state-of-the-art gadgetry and techniques used in crime investigations—DNA analysis and all that—the shovel remained the fire detective's perfect instrument for unearthing clues. Fire cops, no matter if they're federal BATF experts or not, are diggers first before they're anything else.

"I'll assemble a response team before this afternoon," Hamilton promised McAllister.

"Fuhrman and I'll have it solved before you feds can wade through the paperwork and red tape," McAllister chided. He was to regret making *that* careless prediction.

Chapter

5

Carroll County, Virginia

At 9 A.M. on December 5, the Roanoke County pathologist, a rather stocky man with a funereal air and odor, pointed out to Captain Rick Clark what had killed pretty Sheila Ring and her baby daughter. It wasn't fire, he said, and it wasn't smoke inhalation. The lungs of both victims were clear of soot, which meant they had breathed no smoke. The fire had been set to cover up an even more heinous crime.

"They were dead before the fire ever reached them," explained the medical examiner. "They were stabbed to death with a knife. A sharp knife."

The perpetrator, whoever he was, seemed to have gone into a blood frenzy over the nearly nude body of Sheila Ring. Although her charred body concealed and disguised her fatal wounds, it turned out that she had been stabbed all over. Cuts on the forehead, above the right eyebrow, bone-deep lacerations in the back of the skull, on the neck, cuts on the inner thighs and lower torso, some as deep as five inches. There was a gaping stab wound into her back and through her right lung, and more stabs into the genitals.

The little girl, Jasmine, had been treated in the same

manner as the dog outside: her little throat had been sliced to the bone, severing carotid arteries, jugular veins, and her windpipe. Clark's stomach roiled. Like most veteran investigators grown callous to violence committed against adults, he'd never gotten used to seeing victims who were children.

"We have one sick son of a bitch running around in Carroll County," Clark acknowledged.

It was a gray day, cloudy and cold on the drive back to sheriff's headquarters in Hillsville. The little town had one folksy Main Street, a transplanted Mayberry from off the old *Andy Griffith Show* or out of a Norman Rockwell painting. News of the fire and double homicide—plus rumors of a sex fiend–killer hiding in the mountains waiting to strike again—swept the community as fast as the fire devoured Sheila's little house. Locals made a point of stopping anxiously by the sheriff's office to comment and ask questions.

"Are you gonna catch him before he catches another one of us?"

"Just let us do our job," Sheriff Carrico responded.

Investigating a fire-related homicide at this stage was little different from investigating a homicide by gunshot or any other means. It entailed pounding the streets, canvassing for witnesses and asking questions, delving into a victim's background history for some clue as to motive or enemies.

It didn't take the sheriff's men long to determine that Sheila, a single mother for over 2 years who had supported her daughter by working as a sewing machine operator at a local knitting plant, had little contact with her ex-husband, who lived out of state. Spouses, ex-spouses, and lovers were always first suspects in such crimes.

The absence of any life insurance or home owner's policies eliminated the possibility that the murders had been committed to collect fire insurance by some

scheming beneficiary. Carrico and Clark were left looking at a sex angle—say a pyromaniac with a sex kink,
or perhaps the other way around: a sex weirdo with a
pyromania kink.

Whatever, he was running loose out there, perhaps
living quietly and unobtrusively among the citizenry.
His facelessness was making people nervous as hell.
People locked their doors for the first time in memory.

Captain Clark spent that overcast day shoveling
through the ashes at the fire site, searching for a knife
or any other clue to the perpetrator's identity, marking
his measurements and taking photographs for the trial
when—and *if*—the suspect was nabbed. He found only
a singed piece of a brassiere, which he assumed to have
belonged to Sheila. No knife, no footprints, no . . .
nothing. Fire destroyed evidence.

In the meantime, however, the task force of investigators Sheriff Carrico assembled from his 39-man force
was making progress in collecting vital witnesses, the
first of whom was Sheila's neighbor and landlord. From
down the road, if he stepped onto his porch, the
landlord had a view of Sheila's porch and side yard. He
tried to keep an eye open, he said, being as how his
tenant was a single lady living alone with her baby in an
isolated rural location.

It was about 5:30 P.M., about 2 hours or so before the
house erupted in flames on December 3, that he
noticed a yellow compact car parked at Sheila's. A man
on the front porch waved at him—a chunky man with
a buzz-type haircut, a beard, and eyeglasses. He failed
to notice Sheila or her daughter. He said it was the first
time he had seen the man, that he must be a stranger to
the community.

After running out of daylight, Clark gave up his quest
at the fire site and motored back to the jail and sheriff's
headquarters across the street from the stately old brick
county courthouse. He wore jeans, a ball cap, a work

shirt, and coat, all of which, including exposed skin, had turned black from his rummaging around in the ashes at the burn.

Several deputies mingled excitedly in the large open room at headquarters, including Chief Deputy Warren Manning and a couple of other detectives, J. B. Gardner and Steve Williams.

"We got us a suspect," Manning informed the fire cop. "One of the victim's friends told us Sheila was hanky-panky with a character named Midkiff."

"Thomas Jefferson Midkiff? T. J.?"

"You know him?"

"Sheila was messing with that no-good piece of—?"

"Said it had been going on for quite a while, on the sly," another deputy added, "since Midkiff is married. Sheila's landlord identified him from a photo lineup as the same guy he saw messing around her house a couple of hours before the fire."

Looked good. Spouse, ex-spouse, or lover. They were always a good bet.

Captain Clark had known T. J. Midkiff, who was about 27, for the last 5 years. Midkiff was a bit of a character in Carroll County, an itinerant auto mechanic and often a trusty at the Hillsville jail. Folks warned each other not to turn their backs on him and not to leave anything loose that could be stolen when he was around. He had about the longest police record in this part of Virginia. It included, among other crimes, arrests for burglary, attempted rape, malicious wounding, and dealing in marijuana. He was an ex-convict for the burglary conviction.

"The son of a bitch is capable of about anything," Clark opined.

Word went out to field deputies that the sheriff and his fire investigator wanted to question Midkiff about the Ring arson and murders. Clark grabbed a cup of coffee and, since it was still a few minutes before 10 P.M., settled down to wait. Deputies were scouring the county for the suspect; if he was still in the mountains, they would find him. Hillsville pulled in the streets, shut off most of its lights, and locked its doors.

A deputy radioed in at about 10:30 that he had spotted Midkiff's little yellow car headed toward town on State Route 58. Sheriff Carrico picked up the mike of his desk radio. Clark and the other deputies fell silent.

"Keep it under surveillance," Carrico advised the deputy. "See where he goes."

"That's a 10-4, Sheriff."

Midkiff headed for the sheriff's department and parked outside the door. Although it was a crisp night, the husky man with the glasses and pig-bristle head wore only a tank top and jeans as he sauntered in and demanded to see the sheriff. Carrico regarded him patiently from behind his desk.

"I've been hearing you want to talk to me, Sheriff," the intruder began brusquely, "and I come in to see what the hell you wanted."

"There's been a murder—a *double* murder—and a fire," Sheriff Carrico said quietly, studying Midkiff's reactions.

"So?"

"So, I hear you knew her—Sheila Ring."

"I might have, but I don't know nothing about murder. Nothing, Sheriff, and no bastard can say different."

So that was the way he intended playing it? Carrico read Midkiff his Miranda rights, then cajoled him into taking a little ride with him to Virginia State Police headquarters in nearby Wytheville. The sheriff called ahead to have veteran investigator Tolley Svard meet him there. Svard had a reputation as a keen interrogator.

In Wytheville, locked into an interview room with Carrico and Svard, the chunky ex-con took off his glasses, wiped his eyes, and glanced at his watch. It was about 12:45 A.M., December 7, 3 days after the raccoon hunters spotted Sheila's little house blazing.

"If I told you what happened," the man said to the lawmen, "I'd never be able to walk the streets in Hillsville again."

A crack in the guy's mental armor.

"Sheriff Carrico . . . Dick," he said, "I've known you and Rick Clark and some of the others for quite a while. Can I talk to you alone?"

Detective Svard obligingly got up and left but watched the proceedings with Carroll County deputies through a one-way mirror. Carrico bided his time, chatting with the man for a few minutes. The sheriff was a cool man, patient, soft-voiced. Then he fell silent, waiting to let the suspect's conscience work him over some more.

Suddenly, Midkiff's trembling hands sprang from his lap and clawed at his face. He burst into tears.

"Dick, I did it and I need your help. I—I need someone to talk to. I can't live with what's gone on."

"You were over there that night?" the sheriff asked patiently.

"Have I got to answer that, Dick?"

"No, you know your rights. But talk to me, T. J."

Silence, broken only by Midkiff's sniffles.

"Talk to me, T. J."

Finally, the ex-con began talking, but he left out the more gruesome details, glossed over them. It was as if the memory of that night—the rabid stabbing of the woman, the cutting of the throats of the child and dog, setting the woman and child aflame—and what the episode said about him and his character were simply beyond his capability to confront and endure.

"I had an affair with Sheila Ring and she threatened to tell my wife," he said in a low, matter-of-fact voice once his tears subsided. "We broke it off. I went back Tuesday evening. She said, 'Not now. I have company coming.'

"We went into the back bedroom. She took off everything but her bra. Then she said she was going to tell my wife. I lost it, man.

"I hit her and then grabbed the butcher knife. I stabbed her three times and then, as she was falling, I slung the butcher knife again and it got her throat. The kid came running in there and as I turned, I reached out and cut it, too. As I was running out of the house, I took a stick of wood from the stove that was on fire and I threw it back where they was and I ran."

Left unexplained was why he had the butcher knife in the first place. Had he brought it with him? Had he forced Sheila to disrobe at knifepoint? Clark, for one, knew the fire was meant to conceal the crime—one of the several common motives for arson—and had been more deliberately ignited than simply taking a chunk of smoldering wood and throwing it randomly across the room. But . . .

"That's what happened," Midkiff insisted, refusing to face, even perhaps in his own mind, the fury, hate, and other emotions that drove him into committing Carroll County's most heinous crime of the decade.

After the confession, Captain Clark greeted the killer with an amiable "How are you doing, T. J.?"

Midkiff* hung his head. "I've really done it this time, Rick."

---

*Thomas Jefferson "T. J." Midkiff was convicted of two counts of first-degree murder and one count of first-degree arson. He was sentenced to serve, consecutively, two life terms plus 10 years for the arson.

Chapter

6

While fire has played a big role in human culture for at least 30,000 years, used as heat in the winter, to cook food, and as a weapon of attack and defense against animals and other human beings, it has always been instinctively feared. Neglected or misused, it turns from a benign friend into a dreadful enemy.

Arson has been considered barbaric for as long as civilized societies have existed. Ancient Roman law provided severe penalties for arson. Many Christians, blamed for the torching of Rome while Emperor Nero fiddled, were burned to death in Nero's "torture gardens" in retaliation. Evidence suggests that Nero himself may have torched Rome as an excuse to rid himself of political enemies.

If fire is the purifying element, America must rank among the most purified countries on earth. America during the Colonial period was almost morbidly sensitive to cases of arson—and justifiably so. Early America, with its narrow streets and wood construction, was destined to burn and burn again.

America's first arson—as well as the New World's

first arson investigation— occurred in the tiny community of Plymouth Rock a little more than 18 months after the Pilgrims landed in 1620. Flames swept through seven dwellings and a storehouse, destroying much of the settlement's provisions and placing its survival in doubt. William Bradford, one of the colony's leaders, described the evidence.

"For they [the colonists] suspected some malicious dealling, if not plaine treacherie," he wrote. ". . . In the withered leaves whereof the fire was kindled [was] found a longe fire brand of an ell [measure of length—about 45 inches] longe, lying under the wale [wall] on the inside, which could not come their by casualtie [accident], but must be laid ther by some hand . . ."

Some settlers abandoned Plymouth to sail to Jamestown, Virginia, possibly because of the mysterious arsonist dwelling in their midst. Arson in early America prompted the enacting of harsh laws dealing with fire starters. As early as the 1630s, punishment by death could be imposed for the "willful and purposed burning of ships (or) hawses." By 1652, the Massachusetts General Court provided that any individual above the age of 16 convicted of setting fire to "any barn, stable, mill, outhouse, stack of wood, corn or hay or any thing of like nature" could be fined double the value of the destroyed property and be "severely whipt." If the building burned was a dwelling or if injury, death, or great loss of property resulted, the culprit could be sentenced to death and his property seized and given to his victims as compensation.

In Maryland Colony, a convicted arsonist could be hung, have his hand severed from his arm, or be branded on the forehead or hand. A second conviction carried the death penalty.

In spite of such stern penalties, however, greed or lust for vengeance, then as now, drove a number of people to the crime of arson.

On November 19, 1676, the Reverend Increase Mather preached a sermon in which he predicted a fire would create "deplorable desolation" in Boston. The next week, on November 27, just as he foretold, a house near the Red Lion Tavern caught fire and spread quickly, destroying 46 dwellings, several warehouses and stores, and the North Meeting House of Reverend Mather. It has been suggested Mather *knew* the fire would break out and who the firebugs were.

That began a number of arsonist blazes that continued over the next few years. During 1679, incendiaries were quite active, burning barns, hay fields, and a few houses. On August 7, after a previous attempt in May, fire starters succeeded in torching the Sign of the Three Mariners, an alehouse. The fire spread quickly and engulfed at least 80 dwellings and 70 warehouses. In proportion to the town's size and wealth, it was a blaze fully as devastating as the Great Fire of London in 1666.

The Massachusetts General Court passed a resolution banning from the colony a number of people suspected but never convicted of setting the fires. Future incendiaries were promptly and decisively dealt with by the paranoid citizenry. A farmhand was sentenced to 21 years' forced servitude for a man whose barn he burned. A black servant charged and convicted of burning her master's home was "burnt to ashes" on the Boston Commons.

Hard and swift justice continued throughout the later Colonial period. A group of slaves armed themselves in 1712 and set fire to a building in New York. According to the governor, 21 were executed: "Some were burnt, others hanged, one broke on the wheel, and one hung alive in chains in the town, so that there has been the most exemplary punishment inflicted that could be possibly thought of."

At least one black was executed in Boston on July 4, 1723, after being convicted of "maliciously setting on fire a Dwelling House in this Town, in the dead of Night, when the Inhabitants were asleep in their beds."

A series of suspicious fires in New York in 1741, followed by a rumored slave revolt, resulted in the conviction of 113 men and women for arson, most of whom were hanged or burned at the stake.

Motives for arson in early America varied. Revenge was an obvious one. Some fire starters were probably pyromaniacs or thrill seekers. Other fires were likely started in order to cover up felonies, such as murder or theft. Whatever the motive then, it can also be easily found in the modern arsonist. The only motive that was largely absent in early America was the economic one of setting fires to defraud insurance companies, although some early Americans did burn out business competitors, as is still done today.

The idea of fire insurance was first introduced in Flanders in 1240 when a communitywide fire insurance pool was developed to reimburse the losses of one from the resources of the others. Although fire insurance arrived in the New World in 1736, introduced by a firm in South Carolina, it failed because communities lacked an effective way of dealing with fires once they started. Fire insurance was simply not a good risk.

Leave it to the enterprising Ben Franklin to recognize the deficiency and work out a prevention and protection concept to give insurance companies a reasonable expectation of a profit. He established in Philadelphia some of the first truly organized fire brigades. Then, with the means to prevent and fight fires, he founded his own insurance company, which was among the first to use fire marks—molded lead symbols placed on the outside of houses to inform firefighters which insurance firm was responsible to repay losses. Some of these fire marks can still be seen on buildings near George Washington's fire station—Friendship Engine Company #1—in Alexandria, Virginia.

All arson fires, whether in Colonial or modern America and whatever their motivation, can have devastating results, as fire cops know all too well. Creating and maintaining civilized societies involves a struggle in each generation between the forces of barbarism and violence and those of law and decency. Civilization's veneer is often too thin to prohibit some people from following the lure of their baser instincts.

Chapter

7

New York, New York

Some people truly *will* do any goddamned thing.

New York City Special Fire Marshal Louis Garcia followed up on an obvious arson scene in a tiny Manhattan apartment after firefighters extinguished the blaze. Gas fume odors hung thick and oily in the lingering tendrils of smoke and exuded from the remains of charred furniture. Splash patterns delineated where gasoline had been splattered in the living room and ignited. The way Manhattan buildings adjoin one another, the fire could have consumed half the block if a neighbor had not sniffed smoke and dialed 911.

Garcia ordered the tenant, Tony Cozerto, and his live-in girlfriend, Lizette Lopez, to be separated and brought to headquarters for questioning after they got into a scream fight at the scene. The fire marshal brought Cozerto into his office and questioned him first. The man appeared to be hiding something. His knees knocked nervously against the front of the desk while his dark gaze, fueled by anger and frustration, sought refuge in bare corners of the room.

"I know it was that crazy bitch Lizette torched my apartment," Cozerto asserted.

"Did you see her do it?" Garcia asked. The investigator, at a bulky 6 feet 2 inches and over 200 pounds, could sometimes be intimidating. He was pushing 50 and was a Cuban-American, although his accent was consummate New York without a trace of his Spanish heritage. He would soon be promoted to assistant fire chief, making him the highest ranking Hispanic in the history of the New York Fire Department.

Cozerto looked up at him and gulped. "She's been living at my place with me for the last three months," he promptly explained. "I tossed her filthy ass out on the street just this morning—and now somebody lights a match to my place. Who else would do it?"

"You two had a big fight, is that right?"

"Something like that."

"What was the fight about?"

Cozerto stared at the ceiling. The little muscles in his jaws bunched.

"Look, man," he burst out evasively, "I know she did it, okay? So does she."

Curious about what lay behind Cozerto's equivocation and knowing the fire had to be started by either Cozerto or his girlfriend, the fire cop left Cozerto to stew in his anger while he interrogated Lizette in another office. Lizette was a pretty Puerto Rican woman with wonderful deep, dark eyes and a figure that filled out her Levis.

"Your boyfriend is convinced you set the apartment afire," the fire marshal said.

"The *bastard.* I didn't do it, but it would have served him right if I had."

"Let's start from the top. Why did he kick you out of the apartment?"

"It was no big deal. I wanted to go anyhow."

"He was mad at you about something? You were mad at him?"

She chain-smoked filter cigarettes. Her gaze fixed on an ashtray. Her voice softened. "I was mad at him, but

I guess I shouldn't be. Nah, I wasn't really mad, not really."

"But you had a fight? Are you seeing someone else? Is that why you were fighting?"

The girl's eyes snapped at him. "Did he tell you that?"

Garcia shrugged. "I'm asking you. Something must have really pissed him off to kick you out like he did. Has he ever beat you or something?"

"He was good to me; he never touch me," she said, then added with a tiny sarcastic laugh, "And when he *do* touch me, he wasn't no damn good anyhow. Why don't you ask *him* what make him so mad at me?"

She was proving to be as evasive as Cozerto. Garcia continued to play the couple off each other to get to the bottom of the fire starting. They seemed to be of the caliber commonly recruited for daytime tabloid talk shows like *Jerry Springer.*

Returning to Cozerto, Garcia said, "Lizette is pretty angry at you, all right."

Cozerto flared. "That sick fucking bitch! *She's* mad at *me?*"

"She's told me her side," Garcia said, pushing. "I gather she thinks it's all *your* fault. What happened? Did you catch her shacked up with some other dude?"

Cozerto stamped out his cigarette, mutilating it. He laughed bitterly. Funny how his laugh sounded so much like hers.

"Did she tell you it was another dude?" he asked Garcia, punctuating the question with a nasty sound that wasn't quite laughter.

"She's not happy with you as a lover," Garcia said.

Cozerto shook his head in frustration.

"You find her with another *woman?*" the fire cop asked. There were lots of options to pursue in this, the brave new world in which anything and everything goes.

The poor slob's hands shook as he lit another cigarette, then immediately stamped it out.

"Come on, Tony," Garcia pressed. "She humping the grocery delivery boy or what?"

"No, man. No!"

"Another guy in the building? A neighbor?"

"No."

"Maybe some rich guy? Some guy who can buy her more things?"

Cozerto finally exploded from his chair. "That fucking bitch is awful lucky I didn't kill her," he cried.

The guy was ready to break, on the verge. He reseated himself and relit the cigarette he had just extinguished. Garcia leaned back in his chair and watched him.

"Look," Cozerto said. "I know she set my apartment afire 'cause whoever did it had a key and took Butch before she lit the match. Ask her who else got a key. Nobody."

"Who's Butch?"

"Butch ain't some *who*. He's our friggin' dog, our friggin' Doberman."

He squirmed in his chair and blew smoke explosively. His fingertips drummed on the desk. He looked up at Garcia, looked away, looked back, as though trying to make up his mind.

"You know," he said reflectively with a tinge of sadness, "you bring a puppy home and it grows up, and the next thing you know, your girlfriend's boning him."

Garcia stared. He wasn't sure he heard correctly.

"I'm gonna tell you, man," Cozerto said. He faltered. Tears filled his eyes. "Man, when I come home last night . . . when I come home . . ." He let it all out in a rush: "I caught her on the floor with Butch. The bitch fucked my dog, then took him and tried to burn my shit."

He seemed all choked up. He recovered after a moment and said, "Do you think you can find out

44

what she done with Butch? I want my dog back. It ain't his fault."

Garcia stroked his mustache to hide a thin smile. A quarter century on the job had given him the veteran cop's dark sense of humor.

"I'll see what I can do," he promised.* "But you might want to have him fixed before you get another girlfriend."

---

*Neither party was convicted of setting the apartment afire.

Chapter

8

Miami, Florida

Dade County, with its approximately 3,500 square miles of area and its crowded population of more than 2 million people from diverse cultures, might be considered the arson center of America. Each year, greed, passion, and carelessness produces nearly 10,000 fires with a resulting high death toll. Investigations are spearheaded by Captain Rocky McAllister, chief of Metro–Dade Fire Investigations, and Metro Police Detective Wil Fuhrman, supplemented by a BATF National Response Team led by, in the case of the IWDC fire, agent Bill Hamilton.

In fire probes, as in other criminal investigations, detectives often succeed or fail on what they call the 48-hour rule. Essentially, the rule is that most crimes are solved within the first 48 hours after their commission—or they aren't solved at all. Witnesses forget or they move away; evidence is misplaced or destroyed, or loses its value. What good, for example, are plaster casts of footprints at a crime scene after the suspect wears out and trashes the shoes that made the prints?

Some crimes, however, especially major arsons with

extensive damage, can't be accordioned into 48 hours. Fire cops spent at least the first 48 hours of the IWDC probe waiting for the warehouse to cool enough for them to enter and organize it for an on-scene examination. Because of the presence of hazardous chemicals, the federal EPA deployed a hazardous-chemical management team for the cleanup. The team was instructed to be especially aware of the presence of arson evidence as it began clearing pathways for investigators to use to walk through the rubble.

Fuhrman and McAllister scrounged for witnesses among garbage collectors, newspaper delivery people, early birds who worked in the warehouses . . . *somebody* might have noticed something.

"Did you see anyone unusual last night or did anyone come in last night who seemed out of place?" was one of the questions fire cops posed to clerks and waitresses and other night workers at service stations, convenience stores, and cafés in the area.

A clerk at the 7-Eleven off an exit of the Palmetto Expressway gave a cynical laugh. "You're shitting me, right?" he scoffed. "This is *Miami,* man. I been working here two weeks, and I seen 'em come in with green hair and purple hair and no hair. I seen skinny junkies with earrings in their lips and tongues and noses and fat pregnant whores with bleached hair. I seen—"

"We get the point."

"Man, a six-legged Martian with glowing orange eyes and fangs six inches long could stop in here for directions and *he* wouldn't look out of place in Miami."

Much of detective work, whether of a homicide case or any other, involves tedium and wearing out shoe leather. Because of the explosion and the unexplained presence of the fire-melted Realistic walkie-talkie left in the parking lot of the warehouse, detectives had to consider the possibility that the fire starter might have met his death in the holocaust or at least been injured.

Fuhrman and McAllister divided between them the telephone numbers of south Florida hospitals and began calling, asking about fire-injured patients admitted during the early morning hours. Hospitals were required to report suspicious injuries to police, but what was *required* and what actually *happened* were sometimes at opposite poles.

"Nothing at Jackson Memorial," Fuhrman reported to McAllister. "One kid showed up with minor burns and said it was a welding accident. He was sixteen and his father vouched for him."

That was the nearest the fire cops ever came to finding a possible suspect in the hospitals.

Shortly before noon, Fuhrman and McAllister pulled their car up and parked in the driveway of a fine two-story residence in Coral Gables. A maroon Mercedes sat parked in the drive. Automatic sprinklers watered a landscaped lawn as plush as carpet.

"Rami Rabjami is doing well for himself in the U.S. of America," Fuhrman commented out of the deep cynicism of his breed.

The owner of a torched business was always the first suspect. Licenses and other county records listed Rabjami, apparently an immigrant from somewhere in the Far East, as owner of IWDC. A tiny, dark-skinned woman whom the cops assumed to be a Pakistani answered the knock at her door. She was middle-aged and wore a house sarong traditional in her country. Miami was truly the Casablanca of the world.

"Mrs. Rabjami?" Fuhrman inquired.

"The pronunciation is close enough," she replied.

The detectives introduced themselves. McAllister said, "We telephoned the emergency number for your business early this morning to report a fire at your building. No representative from your company has yet showed up that we know of."

Mrs. Rabjami did not invite the men inside. "My husband is out of town," she explained.

"When did he leave?"

"Yesterday morning."

"When will he return?"

"I've notified him of this tragedy. He was heartbroken. He will return to Miami either late tonight or early tomorrow. It is a long flight from New York."

"Maybe you can help us in the meantime?" Fuhrman said. "Are you familiar with the contents of the warehouse and who had merchandise stored there?"

"My responsibility is the house," she responded. "I do know the merchandise varied from time to time. It could be children's toys or washing machines or anything else."

"Electronics? Radios, TVs?"

"Perhaps. I do not know everything."

"One more question. Was there a watchman or anyone else who worked there at night who might have carried a two-way radio?"

"There was no need for anyone to remain there after closing."

Fuhrman gave up. He handed her his card. "Have your husband call us when he returns."

As they left and walked across the green carpet of the lawn to their parked car, Fuhrman rumbled, "We might have foreseen that the warehouse owner would be out of town when it happened——establishing an alibi?"

Fire detectives scraped and poked around inside the warehouse for several days, looking for clues and evidence, like field mice digging for kernels of corn in a barn.

"What we need to look for," McAllister commented, only half joking, "is an arm with a hand clutching a cigarette lighter and the rest of a walkie-talkie."

They established several facts first off. Since there were no signs of forced entry or burglary, the intruder—if indeed the fire *was* arson, as it appeared—must have had a key or other method of entering the building without setting off the burglar alarm; that meant an *inside* job. An employee, perhaps?

Fact two: the intruder must have used a timer to allow him or her opportunity to escape before the building blew. Either that, or the starter had gone up with the building.

"Going in there using an accelerant to set a fire without a delayed timing device," opined Fuhrman, "is like going into battle and shooting yourself with your own weapon."

"Maybe he *did* shoot himself—and now his partner has tossed him into Biscayne Bay or the Miami River," Hamilton suggested.

Fuhrman acted as safety outside the building while McAllister donned his space suit getup—heavy turnouts and boots, fire hat, SCBA, two-way radio—and entered the giant pile of charred rubble. It was gloomy inside, still filled with slowly oozing smoke. Visibility was limited to about 15 feet. Timbers, metal containers, and other unidentified black things littered the building, and McAllister climbed over them, stumbling and supporting himself with gloved hands, using a wide-lens flashlight to illuminate his way. The place was like a sauna. Even through his boots, he felt the heat of the pooled oil-slick puddles of water. Sweat rolled and squished in his armpits and crotch.

Like most fire cops, he carried around some knowledge of a dozen specialties to aid him in his inspection. He knew a little about building construction, some about sprinkler systems, and some more about electrical systems. He understood a great deal about fuel loads and venting and the elements of the fire triangle—fire, heat, oxygen—and how they interacted to form particular burn patterns. He knew flame behavior under different weather conditions, how fire reacted to various kinds of cloth, masonry, wood, glass, paper, metals, fluids, and gases.

For example, he knew it was nearly impossible for a cigarette to start a grass fire in humidity above 23%. He knew how slow, smoldering fires deposited smoke on glass panes and cracked them in a spiderweb pattern but fast-burning fires created an explosive rush and blew glass apart before smoke could glaze them. He knew that incandescent light bulbs expanded *toward* intense heat so that they actually pointed out the origin of fire. He also knew that all substances known to man can burn if the right amount of heat was applied.

He looked for all these signs inside the warehouse, along with fire cones, heat lines, trailer marks, accelerant residue, char depth and color, areas of most destruction. The body of a full-grown bull elephant could have been lost among such debris.

"Christ, it's a mess in here," he radioed Fuhrman.

He determined that flashpoint had occurred almost simultaneously at several different locations within the central section of the football field–size warehouse. It had ignited suddenly, explosively, an all-but-certain indicator of arson, strengthening the fire cop's conviction that *this* was an act of man, not of God.

Repeatedly losing his footing in the wreckage, he stumbled and fell in what appeared to be a small field of 5-gallon hard-plastic jugs, many of which had endured the blaze. The fall dislodged his face mask. He replaced it quickly as his flashlight beam danced across the jugs, most of which had had their caps removed. Blue lettering identified the contents of the jugs as kerosene.

Kerosene is slow burning; it couldn't have been the accelerant that produced *this* explosion and fire. Nonetheless, McAllister selected one of the jugs to carry out with him. It contained some liquid residue.

His right arm and forehead, which had made contact

with foreign material when he fell, dislocating his face shield and exposing one arm above his glove, began to burn as though under attack by a horde of fire ants. One eye was already swelling shut by the time he lunged into fresh air outside on the docking apron.

"Something toxic is in these jugs," he cried, "and it's not kerosene! There are dozens of them in there, all mostly emptied with their tops off."

Chapter

9

Craig, Alaska

There are two ways to get to Craig——by boat or by airplane. No roads lead off Prince of Wales Island to mainland North America in the far south panhandle of Alaska. Knee-deep in the cold blue Pacific, the tiny fishing village, population 1,000, faces outward past several other smaller, largely deserted islands to the open Gulf of Alaska. The main industry in Craig, other than the fishing boats at the piers, was the fish cold-storage plant and cannery. It was often gray, wet country where, it was said, halibut and salmon might live as well outside the ocean as in it.

On the morning of September 6, a Monday, the 57-foot *Investor,* captained by Mark Coulthurst out of Bellingham, Washington, pulled out of dock in Craig later than the other fishing vessels. It was toward the middle of salmon season and most captains liked to be on the fishing grounds before first light, where they stayed for days at a time until they filled their holds.

Fishing had been good for *Investor* since she arrived on the island 2 weeks previously. On Saturday, the trawler had steamed in with 70,000 pounds of prime salmon and warped to the disabled *Decade,* since there were no other berths available. *Decade* was waiting on parts to be shipped up from Seattle. Coulthurst decided to lay over on Sunday instead of fishing, since it was his birthday. He promised to take his wife Irene and their 5-year-old daughter Kimberly and 4-year-old son John out to the only *real* restaurant in Craig to celebrate.

The *Investor,* a new $800,000 vessel constructed to Coulthurst's specs, was the only craft in the harbor containing every possible safety device, enough electronics equipment and radio-telephones to allow the craft to cross the Pacific either physically or by communication, high guardrails, and a playground on the foredeck with swings and teeter-totters.

The Coulthursts, including their children, lived aboard the trawler during salmon season.

"I'm a fisherman, but that doesn't mean I can't have a family life too," big Mark Coulthurst often declared.

Coulthurst was a burly, genial man of 27, with dark hair below the collar of his oilskins and a black mustache. Fishing was his life. His first fishing boat, which he acquired when he was 16, was a wooden skiff with oars. He used castoff nets to catch herring for their imitation caviar eggs in the Strait of Juan de Fuca off Bellingham. Gradually, saving his money, he advanced to an outboard for the skiff, then to an old rusted trawler, and finally, when he was still a young man, to the boat of his dreams—the *Investor.*

"Hey, the bank and I are worth darned near a million bucks," he would exclaim, grinning into the salt spray from his flying bridge. At 4 years old, little John was often with him topside, dressed in his own miniature oilskins.

"I gonna be a fisherman——like my daddy," he would say when asked his life's ambition.

On that Monday in Craig when the *Investor* got her late start, still in the gray of dawn but after daybreak and therefore late, the idle crew of the *Decade* casually noticed that the trawler was using her auxiliary motor underway. Instead of throwing up her big heavy wake across the flat morning bay, she chugged along slowly. Only one person appeared visible on the boat, he at the helm.

She had also, oddly enough, tossed her tie-lines onto the *Decade*'s deck. Tie-lines are heavy, braided rope, each of which cost $100 or more. No fishing boat discards them lightly.

Later that morning, other fishing boats noticed *Investor* lazily riding her anchor on a small, deep bay at Egg Island, about a mile cross-sea from Craig and within view of the village as long as the fog remained above mast level. None of the passing fishing boats noticed anyone on deck anytime during the day.

They observed no one aboard on Tuesday, until around 4:30 P.M.

The captain of the *Casino* had made up his mind that morning to check out the *Investor* if she was still at anchor off the island when he returned to harbor in the evening. While his own ship was still over a mile out, he and his mate observed a skiff with one person in it leaving the trawler. The skiff kicked up a rooster tail as it sped for Craig.

"That ain't like Mark to be sitting out good fishing days," Captain Don Shields observed, frowning. "But, hell, I guess he knows what he's doing."

Partly reassured by the sight of the man in the skiff, Shields nonetheless kept on course to pass at the mouth of the bay in which *Investor* rode. *Casino* throttled back; her wake lapped gently at the island's rocky shore and bobbed *Investor*. The boat looked abandoned in the gray twilight.

Suddenly, from somewhere inside her bowels, the boat belched a phlegmish wad of black-gray smoke, followed by a flickering red tongue of flame. Nothing was more feared in the icy waters of Alaska than fire aboard ship at sea. The only escape was to go overboard—and survival, even with the proper gear, was a slim proposition in the freezing saltwater.

Within mere seconds, the entire length of the 57-footer turned into a blazing Viking's pyre, forcing *Casino* to withdraw. Captain Shields chopped a Mayday call to the Coast Guard stationed at Ketchikan.

"Thank God, there was nobody aboard," he radioed. "Somebody was leaving in a skiff, and we saw no one else on her."

There were two Coast Guard vessels in Craig, neither of which was equipped with firefighting apparatus. They asked for help from Ketchikan, which dispatched a seaplane loaded with two large pumps. The plane made the 60-mile strip in less than a half hour, landed, and quickly transferred the pumps to the tug *Andy Head*.

Investor had burned almost to the waterline by the time the first streams of water landed on her. Only an elaborate sprinkler system kept the fire from exploding the belowdecks diesel tanks. By sunset, the boat had turned into a charred, blackened wreck, with part of her superstructure burned and dropped into the hull. But she still floated—barely.

The skipper of *Andy Head* sent a crewman aboard the still-smoking deck to lift anchor so the tug could tow her to shallow water. Moments after jumping onto the hot deck, the crewman ran to the railing and vomited.

"What's going on? What's the trouble?" the skipper shouted.

"There's people aboard!" the crewman gasped.

"How many?"

"God, I don't know. They're stacked up like hamburgers on a grill and fried to a crisp."

Chapter

10

Detectives investigating a homicide understand that the least reliable method of identifying a dead body is by direct visual examination, sometimes called "gross examination." Under stress, grieving observers simply cannot seem to identify a loved one. There have been numbers of instances of misidentification.

Equally unreliable is identification by clothing and personal effects—jewelry, religious medals, name belts, wallets with ID cards. Such identification is especially untrustworthy in deaths involving fire, since the victim's personal effects might have been damaged or consumed and the victim rendered virtually featureless.

For that reason, fire investigators depend upon coroners, medical examiners, dentists, doctors, and even anthropologists to identify victims. There are at least seven methods of identification based upon characteristics of the deceased compared with his or her known predeath traits.

In disasters with a large number of bodies, such as the 81 incurred as a result of the shootout and fire at the Branch Davidian stronghold in Waco, Texas, the

first separations are made on the characteristics of sex. Male bodies may be further separated into circumcised or uncircumcised groups. Even when bodies are almost consumed by fire, sex may still be determined through examination of the torso. Deep-seated organs in the pelvic region—the male prostate, female uterus—are usually among the last organs to be destroyed by fire.

Probably the most positive means of identifying a corpse is through fingerprints—if the victim's hands and fingers have not already been burned away. The FBI established its national fingerprint file in 1924, which today contains the prints of millions of Americans. Crime-scene technicians may obtain a cadaver's prints at the scene, or they can remove the skin of the hand or even the hand itself and submit it to the laboratory for analysis.

A victim's teeth remain after most of the body's soft flesh has disintegrated into ashes. Not only may teeth be compared with the dental records and X rays of a victim of a suspected arson fire to confirm identity, but they also provide, in the case of unknown victims, important information regarding age, race, preexisting diseases, habits, socioeconomic conditions, and even, occasionally, occupation. For example, seamstresses often wear their teeth in a particular manner by cutting thread with their teeth; a boxer's teeth may be broken and loosened in the jaw.

Since skeletal bones resist the wear of environmental conditions, time, and heat, trained anthropologists can analyze them to determine the victim's age and height at time of death, sex, race, and evidence of prior disease and even to distinguish between animal and human bones. Some anthropologists successfully recreate a dead person's facial features from the skull or portions of it.

Blood, tissue, and hair remains may provide meth-

ods of identification through blood groupings and Rh types, sex chromatin, karyotyping, and DNA analysis and comparison.

Even on a badly charred cadaver, postmortem examination—autopsy—often reveals such distinctive characteristics as occupational scars and marks, evidence of preexisting diseases or injuries, congenital defects, surgical scars, and the absence of organs due to surgeries. An autopsy can also determine whether a finger or limb was amputated prior to a fire or was lost in the blaze. It can even determine that the victim had had tattoos, although the arm itself that bore the tattoo might be burned off.

Take, for example, the body of a badly burned man known to have a DEATH BEFORE DISHONOR tattoo on his left arm. The arm has been burned off. The pathologists may locate traces of the tattoo ink deposited in the lymph glands of the left armpit, where it had been absorbed into the body.

Radiography is the seventh method of identification. Organ and bone X rays taken during life can be compared with postmortem films. Known fractures, splintered bones, and other such injuries the victim might have incurred in life will show up in postmortem x-ray images, as will foreign materials and metallic fragments, such as shrapnel from mortar explosions or unremoved bullets.

Most fire victims die from carbon monoxide poisoning, not from thermal exposure. Only rarely do people actually *burn* to death. Two pounds of cotton waste burned inside a relatively large room rapidly develops a lethal level of carbon monoxide. Absence of carbon in the blood of a dead body found inside a burned structure and absence of soot in the nose, throat, larynx, and trachea is strong circumstantial evidence that the person was dead—and therefore possibly murdered—before the fire began.

Fire may be used as a weapon in homicide or as a means to cover up the crime. Whichever the use, the identity of the victim must first be legally established, along with the method of his or her death, in order for a suspect to be charged with murder.

Chapter

11

Craig, Alaska

Wednesday dawned gray with a sheen of mist off the sea. It lacquered the black char of the *Investor* where the boat had been beached on the rocky shore outside the town. The *skree! skree!* of seagulls and the darting black-winged terns greeted veteran detectives Lieutenant John Shover and Sergeant Charles Miller as they rode their thick-soled hiking boots along the beach to the dead boat with its cargo of dead bodies, number unknown. Coroner Kris Carlisle from Ketchikan and his deputies were on their way over by boat.

The Alaskan state police had placed Shover and Miller in charge of the investigation; each had received the call last night from dispatch.

"It's a fishing boat burned to the gunnels," dispatch explained briefly. "It has the cremated remains of an unknown amount of people aboard. The Coast Guard has had it beached at Craig and will guard the crime scene until state troopers take over."

Alaskan law-enforcement officers, like the rest of the citizens of that far north state, were hardy outdoor folk, scattered far apart across the land, and versatile enough

61

to handle all situations. Few law officers in those circumstances were specialists; Shover, for example, had investigated virtually every crime from bear poaching to homicide during his long career in the north woods. He and Miller had each received some training in arson investigations. That and their reputations as competent and tireless homicide dicks made them the best fire cops available to probe the whodunit of the charred corpses left aboard the ghost boat *Investor.*

Their first inquiry was to learn how many people were aboard the boat and their identities. At the same time, they dispatched detectives around town to find out exactly who it was the crew of the *Casino* saw fleeing the fishing vessel in the skiff just prior to the fire. How difficult could it be, on a sparsely inhabited island surrounded by freezing Arctic-like waters, to locate him and give him a name?

Yet Alaska is a big country. People mind their own business there. It's so easy to get lost there.

Talking it over, putting together the known facts, the two grizzled lawmen formed a plausible scenario to explain the crime. They concluded the murders likely occurred in Craig over the weekend, not while the boat was anchored at Egg Island. Add it up, Shover suggested; the tie-lines hurriedly left behind as *Investor* pulled out of dock Monday morning—*late;* a single man seen at the boat's helm and none on deck as *Investor* steamed slowly away; the anchoring for over 40 hours next to an all but deserted island with no persons seen aboard all that time by passing fishing boats, other than late Tuesday afternoon when the skiff scurried away.

If it was indeed an arson-murder, the arson was probably an afterthought, to cover up an even more heinous crime.

It soon became apparent that the fire could not have started accidentally. Evidence revealed flames had erupted simultaneously from a number of places on the vessel—and explosively. An accelerant was used, no doubt.

It was grim work digging into the ashes. The coroner and his deputies first examined a stack of corpses in the boat's galley. The remains, burned bacon-crisp, were melded into a black chunk of charcoal, bones, teeth, and metal. The bodies were removed in a single, greatly reduced lump from what they must have been in life.

"How many are there?" Lieutenant Shover asked Carlisle the coroner.

"I can't say for sure." Carlisle shook his head. "Three, four . . . maybe more."

"And children?" Shover asked.

"At least two. There are more bodies belowdeck."

Shover had seen violent death during his years with the state police, but never before had he witnessed murder on such a large scale. All these people . . . seven, eight, maybe more. Dead. And it was his job to find out why, how, and at the hands of whom. He stared away into space and shook his head. The enormity of the crime suddenly weighed heavily on him.

Belowdecks was even worse. Mostly there was just bones, some teeth, and barbecued pieces of flesh. Parts of the human remains might have been sucked out into the bay when the tug pumped water from the hull so it could be towed in and beached. Officers painstakingly recorded the location of each body part recovered and photographed and bagged it for later identification attempts. Here again, there was no way of determining how many people had been incinerated belowdecks. The amount and location of grisly remains suggested there were at least three or four people and that they might have been in their berths when the fire consumed them.

Officers carried sagging black body bags and sacks of ashes and other debris off the boat until far into the night. Ashes would be sifted for evidence. Cops and coroner deputies alike were black from the char and they stank of wood smoke, diesel fuel, and death.

Shover was in the local constabulary's office, on the telephone to a Coulthurst relative in Bellingham, when a trooper burst in with the news that the skiff from the *Investor* had been located, beached, and abandoned down the shoreline from the cold-storage plant. A small crowd of curious onlookers was gathered outside the office. Shover motioned the trooper to close the door. He covered the phone mouthpiece with his thick palm.

"It was rammed up on the beach, like it hit at full speed," the trooper said. "We've got the crime lab going over it now and we're trying to find witnesses who might have seen the driver."

Shover nodded and returned to his long-distance conversation.

"I talked to Mark Sunday on his birthday," the relative was saying, trying to be helpful in spite of his sorrow. "Irene and the babies, I know, were aboard with him. He didn't say anything about any of the original crew having left him or that he had hired any new crew.

"Now, look. Mark was a real stickler about fire danger. He allowed diesel aboard because he had no other choice. Other than that, he wouldn't permit gasoline, alcohol, or propane. He wouldn't even allow cigarette lighters. He was afraid of fire."

The detective hung up after promising to inform the relative of new developments. He stared at a memo pad on the desk in front of him. Listed on the pad were names, ages, last-known addresses, and some shorthand particulars on eight people who *should* have been aboard *Investor* when she sailed out of Craig on Monday morning:

Mark Coulthurst, 27, captain
Irene Coulthurst, 27, wife
Kimberly Coulthurst, 5, daughter
John Coulthurst, 4, son
Michael Stewart, 19, Mark's cousin, sophomore at Washington State University, third-year crew member
Dean Moon, 19, from Mark's hometown in Blaine, Washington, high-school football star, planned to enter Washington State U in the fall
Jerome Keown, 19, honor student at Seattle University
Chris Heyman, 18, new crew member, son of Mark's close friend who owns a marina in San Rafael, California

Lieutenant Shover rubbed his face wearily. He gazed out through the window over the heads of the hangers-on outside. The long Alaskan summer days were starting to get shorter. A fishing trawler chugged across the slick gray waters of the bay, inbound for the docks. A rain squall skipped along the horizon, merging sea and sky.

It was doubtful at this point if the coroner would ever be able to determine if there were eight people aboard *Investor,* or seven or even six. Not enough of the bodies remained.

Which of these eight people—*six* actually, excluding the two children—was *not* aboard when the trawler exploded in flames? Which had not been seen around Craig afterward—except perhaps while fleeing in the skiff?

Chapter

12

New York, New York

Environment, social conditions, economics, class, population—all are factors influencing the amount, type, and nature of crimes committed. Alaska, for example, is a virtual wilderness outside her three or four large cities, a sparsely populated land of fishermen, hunters, and other outdoors types. That state's worst mass murder occurred, quite predictably, outdoors, on a fishing boat, the *Investor,* isolated on the high seas, near a wind-swept island—and the toll was somewhere between six and eight persons. Fire was involved.

On the other hand, the largest mass murder in American history, until the Oklahoma City bombing of the Alfred P. Murrah Federal Building in 1995, occurred in densely populated New York City, inside a nightclub on a crowded boulevard. Fire was the weapon, and it claimed 87 lives, the second highest fire loss in U.S. history. By a macabre twist of irony, the fire was set on the seventy-ninth anniversary of the Triangle Shirtwaist Company fire in which 146 young garment workers were accidentally burned to death. It also occurred in New York and was the highest fire loss in the nation's history.

The first pushout alarm rang in firehouses at 3:41 A.M. on Sunday, March 25: a blaze, with casualties, at the Happy Land Social Club at 1959 Southern Boulevard in the Bronx. Engine Company 45 and Ladder Company 58 were among the first of a dozen to arrive at the scene of mass carnage, above which hung the pungent stench of gasoline. It wasn't a large blaze in terms of actual flame; firefighters had it knocked down within 5 minutes. The real damage was in the loss of lives.

Firefighters and emergency medical workers told the grisly story.

"There was someone in the street who was telling us there were loads of people trapped inside," said one firefighter from Engine Company 45. "Yet we couldn't hear anybody screaming. We didn't hear any yelling. There was no one hollering.

"As we made our way up to the second floor, it was just layers of bodies. They were intertwined and contorted and fused together from the heat. We had to untangle them.

"You can't imagine what went on in there. You can't imagine what those people did to try to survive."

A firefighter from Ladder Company 58 added, "Some looked like they were sleeping. Some looked horrified. Some looked like they were in shock. There were some people holding hands. There were some people who looked like they were trying to commiserate and hug each other. Some people had torn their clothes off in their panic to get out."

Still another stunned firefighter gave his impressions, saying, "You see the first body and you say, 'We didn't get here fast enough.' Then you see the second body, and the third body, and the fourth body, and after that you can't talk anymore. There's nothing to say."

"When I got there," said an emergency medical technician (EMT), "there were already nineteen people piled up outside on the sidewalk. Some looked like they had tried to get their coats over their heads to protect their faces. There was one woman who looked like she was trying to hold onto her boyfriend for dear life. There was a woman holding onto the hand of a man she was with. There was a man lying over a woman as if he was trying to shield her with his body. I had to count and tag every one of those bodies. My head is still spinning."

New York Police Lieutenant James Malvey of the 48th Precinct was assigned immediately, phone-jangled out of bed, to investigate the arson with the city fire marshal and his fire detectives.

"After 25 years on the force," Malvey commented, "I thought I had seen just about everything. I hadn't—until that night. I had never seen carnage like that."

Uniformed police set up lines on Southern Boulevard and East Tremont Avenue, beyond which they lay out the sheet-covered corpses of the dead from the nightclub. Representatives from the medical examiner's office tagged them and prepared them for removal to morgues. Ultimately, police counted 87 of them—more casualties than had occurred in Vietnam during most single battles. Survivors, friends, and relatives piled into the street to add to the bedlam with their shrieks, screams, and wailing.

The neighborhood around the Social Club, as it was commonly called, was composed primarily of Honduran nationals and immigrants. Most of the victims were either Hondurans from the economically deprived community on Southern Boulevard or other Latinos from nearby projects. In time, fire cops learned that only five people managed to escape the club alive once the fire started. Twenty-six of the dead were women; 61 were men. Of the casualties, 68 were removed from the upper floor of the two-story structure, 19 from the narrow stairway to the ground floor. Most died from carbon monoxide poisoning and smoke inhalation; a number of others perished under the crush of the weight of bodies falling on them in the panic to flee the fire.

The building itself was a fire trap with only one exit—down the narrow stairway to the door. It was decrepit, graffiti-mottled. The club itself was clandestine, unlicensed by the city—a juke joint, a "blind pig." Illegal. Simply waiting for a tragedy.

It didn't take long for police detectives and fire cops working under Lieutenant Malvey's command to pick up a thread as to what might have happened. A small crowd of people, including one of the club's bouncers, had knotted up either in the club's entrance or on the street immediately outside before the blaze erupted. These people were eager to tell detectives what they had witnessed. Taking their statements occupied officers until nearly noon Sunday.

About a half hour before the fire began, fire cops learned, a screaming fight broke out between a man and a woman inside the makeshift nightclub. The bouncer finally grabbed the man, wrestled him to the front door, and ejected him. The man was in his thirties, was thick-chested, and had long, greasy hair and a beard—either a Honduran, Puerto Rican, or of other Spanish origin.

"Don't push me! Don't push!" he kept shouting as he was tossed unceremoniously into the street.

He turned on the sidewalk outside and shouted furiously, "I'll be back. I'll shut this place down."

At 3 A.M., a college student working his first night of a part-time job at a neighborhood self-service gas station sold a bearded man a dollar's worth of gasoline in a plastic container. No one saw the man who tossed gasoline into the entrance of the club and ignited it. The old dry lumber in the building went up like an explosion, trapping most of the occupants upstairs and in the stairwell.

The woman involved in the screaming fight had left the club before the fire. Malvey traced her through acquaintances to a low-rent project in the neighborhood. Her ex-boyfriend's name, she said— the name of the thick-chested hombre with the beard—was Julio Gonzalez, 36 years old.

"He told me when we was fighting, he say to me, 'You won't be here tomorrow.' Then he got throwed out."

Julio Gonzalez, it turned out, was a Cuban refugee—a member of the infamous Mariel boat-lift of Fidel Castro's unwanted criminals and psychopaths whom President Jimmy Carter had permitted to enter the United States 10 years before. He had served time in a Cuban prison as an army deserter, then had been housed in a detention camp at Fort Chaffee, Arkansas, upon his arrival in the United States. He stayed there for a year before his release to a sponsor in New York. Now, Gonzalez, like most of the *Marielistos,* had become involved in a serious crime in the United States.

Crimes didn't come much more serious than mass murder.

At 4 P.M. Sunday, Lieutenant Malvey rapped on Gonzalez's door in the Bronx. With him were two police detectives and an assistant fire marshal. The bearded Cuban national appeared sleepy-eyed at the door.

"We need to ask you some questions," Malvey said, flashing his shield. "Down at the station house."

For all Gonzalez's concern, he could have been arrested on traffic warrants.* "Do you have a cigarette?" he asked casually on the drive to the precinct station.

---

*Julio Gonzalez confessed and was charged with having committed the biggest mass murder in United States history up to that point. In all, he was arraigned on 87 counts of murder committed in the course of arson, 87 counts of murder with depraved indifference to human life, one count of attempted murder, and two counts of arson. He was sentenced to multiple life terms in prison.

Chapter

13

Miami, Florida

The IWDC fire was not a loss-of-life fire—at least not that the fire cops were aware of at first. It was, however, turning into a genuine whodunit, what Bill Hamilton called a "small print" case, meaning it was intricate, involved, requiring minute attention to detail. The time requirement of the 48-hour rule ran out quickly and already the case was seeming to stretch into forever—one of those cases in which arrest and conviction, if they took place in the investigators' lifetime, occurred as a result of adding up thousands of scraps of information and evidence.

Rami Rabjami, the building's owner, remained away from home, along with his inventory records, bills, insurance documents, and other papers Hamilton's audit team required in order to shed light on who might have the most to gain from the fire. *Cui bono?* was the Latin phrase for it. *Cui bono?* Who benefits?

Attempts to trace the discarded Realistic walkie-talkie led to Radio Shack, which had literally sold a million of the damned things. No other two-way radios had turned up inside the warehouse. Neither had investigators found remains of a timer or detonator, although laboratory analysis revealed that an accelerant had been used, and used liberally, starting in the north-center section of the structure where Rocky McAllister uncovered the toxic chemical jugs that sent him to the emergency department for skin injuries.

"Why would a torch need to communicate anyhow?" Detective Fuhrman argued over the importance of the walkie-talkie. "For that matter, he might not have needed a timer either. All he had to do was duck inside, strike a match, and run back out. Presto! Instant bonfire."

"How about an answer to this question?" McAllister countered. "How did the fire starter get two or three hundred jugs of accelerant into the warehouse to get the fire started?"

"Hey, you have to do some of the work."

McAllister shrugged. "Maybe they were already inside," he said.

The warehouse sat upon a slight rise in the terrain. Not exactly a hill—the highest elevation in the area was Mount Trashmore, the county dump—but still enough of a rise that runoff water nasty with residue from whatever accelerant had been used had drained into a street gutter, trickled two blocks in the direction of Miami International Airport, crossed a sward of weed-infested greenery, and squeezed into a small lake next to a flamingo-pink jumble of apartment complexes. Some kid rode a Jet Ski on the lake.

"Is that stuff harmful to people using the lake?" McAllister wondered aloud.

"Not as diluted as it is," Hamilton said. "Besides, how are you going to keep kids out of the lake—post armed guards? All the little lakes around Miami are three-fourths chemicals and only one-fourth water anyhow."

HazMat and BATF recovered a total of 64 5-gallon jugs still in decent condition, plus the remains of as many as 200 more. Perhaps it was only coincidence, but it seemed to McAllister that the "kerosene" containers marked what may have been the primary target for destruction. Rabjami, when he returned, would have to clarify which of his business clients had merchandise stored in that particular area.

The manufacturer's name on the "kerosene" vessels was CanChem. So far, the response team had come up empty-handed in attempts to locate such a company. It simply did not exist in the United States.

In addition to the CanChem jugs, the response team salvaged several drums of medicinal-smelling liquid, which the BATF lab in Atlanta quickly identified as Acticide, a pesticide with a water base that steams under heat but does not burn. The lab identified the CanChem residue as acetone.

Acetone—chemical makeup C_3H_6O—is nasty stuff. It is a destructive distillation of wood spirits and various other organic compounds with a bitter taste and a strong wood smoke odor. Commercial labs use it in making chloroform and as a solvent for fats, camphors, and resins. It is also good for getting a bonfire up and going.

Hamilton followed the piercing beam of his flashlight through the gloom and dust and drifting ash of the dead IWDC building to the point of the fire's origin. He stood there in deep thought with McAllister. Sunlight swirled in a bar of golden motes through an opening high in the roof, illuminating a single large square where the CanChem containers had been concentrated.

"Acetone is a controlled substance," Hamilton explained, "in that legally, you can't buy it in large quantities without the seller's keeping records on who buys it and where it goes."

McAllister frowned.

Hamilton shrugged. "I'm no chemist, so I don't know exactly how it's used legally—but dope smugglers process cocaine with it."

McAllister whistled underneath his breath. That revelation threw another factor into the equation. "A thousand or more gallons of acetone is a lot of cocaine processing," he said, awed.

The BATF agent nodded. "We're talking big money here. *Cartel* money, most likely. I don't know what we're into here, partner, but it's starting to look heavy."

Chapter

14

Craig, Alaska

Like the IWDC case in Miami, the investigation of the *Investor* mass murder also seemed to stretch into forever. The grim task of attempting to identify the remains continued in the Ketchikan medical examiner's office while Lieutenant Shover and his men on Prince of Wales Island pursued the lead of the abandoned skiff and how the suspect might have gotten off the island—if indeed he *had* gotten off.

The bodies of Mark, Irene, and Kimberly Coulthurst were positively identified. However, there wasn't enough left of 4-year-old John to say positively that it was his little bones found among those of his parents and sister.

"I have more news for you," the medical examiner (ME) radio-telephoned Shover. "Both adults had been shot through their skulls, execution-style."

It was known that Mark kept a .223-caliber rifle aboard his fishing trawler. Troopers sifting through ashes recovered the melted remains of what had been a rifle, but there was no possible way of proving whether it was the murder weapon.

Only one of Coulthurst's dead crew members had so

far been identified: Michael Stewart, Coulthurst's cousin. That left Dean Moon, Jerome Keown, and Chris Heyman unaccounted for.

"There aren't enough teeth, bones, or skulls to be certain of identity," the ME apologized. "I simply don't know how many remains we have or who they are. At this point, they could be virtually *anybody*. There could be two of them—or there could be four of them. Maybe more."

Because of this inability to name the bones, Lieutenant Shover had no choice but to consider crew members Moon, Keown, and Heyman as potential suspects—at least *one* of them might be a killer. He dispatched trooper-investigators to Washington to locate relatives and friends of the three young men. It was a double-pronged mission.

"Determine if they've been seen since the fire," Shover instructed. "Determine what kind of men they were and if they had a reason to murder Mark Coulthurst."

In the meantime, state investigators literally shut off Prince of Wales Island from the mainland. Troopers patrolled the docks, asking questions of fishermen and crews. They ranged into the rugged interior of the 100-mile-long island, searched the coastlines. Shover was a tireless, broad-shouldered outdoorsman in his forties; nevertheless, working from sunrise until well into the soggy Alaskan nights left him beat. Dark circles formed underneath his eyes. Hot coffee and sheer willpower kept him going. A lot of media attention was focused on this, the "biggest one-time crime in Alaskan history," as it was labeled. Even the normally indefatigable senior detective felt pressure from the media, his superiors, citizens, and even the governor to solve this thing—and soon.

Three witnesses who saw the man in the skiff helped narrow the search to a single description. Ed Dupew, a crusty fishing hand whose craft was beached for repairs, spotted the *Investor*'s skiff scooting into the harbor. He thought it a little odd at the time that the fellow cut his outboard only at the last moment and let the little boat's momentum drive it hard upon the beach at the edge of town. Most small boats tied up at the wharves.

A slender young man jumped out of the boat and hurried away.

"I'd say he was about eighteen or nineteen, maybe in his early twenties," Dupew recollected when he voluntarily came in to tell Shover and his men what he saw. "Let's see . . . brown hair two or three inches below his ears. He was wearing blue jeans with a red-and-black jacket, rectangle-shaped eyeglasses, and a blue baseball cap."

Moon and Keown were 19, Heyman 18.

"Did you know him?" Shover inquired, leaning forward across his desk. "Did you recognize him?"

"Now, Sheriff—"

"It's Lieutenant; I'm not the sheriff."

"Now, Lieutenant, you know how it is out here during fishing season when the cannery is going full blast and all the fishing boats are working. Why, there're more transients out here during salmon season than there are *real* people. The population of Craig more than doubles and I know hardly anybody in town then."

There were, indeed, a lot of salmon strangers on the island. It was a difficult task, determining who had recently arrived in Craig and who had left. Fishing boats entered and left port in a steady stream when salmon were running, coming in to dump their catches at the cold-storage plant or cannery, then rushing back to sea. A year's salary had to be made during those few weeks at the end of the short summer.

The other two witnesses were cannery workers who happened to be on Cole Island, which is next to Egg

Island, on the day the trawler exploded in flames. They were doing a little youthful exploring. The skiff, they insisted, had made an earlier trip ashore, then returned, before it was seen fleeing *Investor* minutes before fire broke out. Their description of the boatman matched that provided by Ed Dupew, the fishing hand.

Lieutenant Shover called in a police artist, who worked with the witnesses to produce a likeness of a slender, young, bespectacled suspect wearing a cap. He looked a little nerdish in the sketches that soon papered the windows of airstrip hangars, marinas, restaurants, and bars on the island as well as in the mainland city of Ketchikan. Fishermen both in Alaska and the Puget Sound area of Washington where Coulthurst had based himself began subscribing to a reward fund. Reward flyers reached as far north as Point Barrow in the Arctic circle and as far south as San Diego.

"We can't sit on our soft duffs and wait for somebody to come to us," Lieutenant Shover warned during morning strategy meetings at the local police station. "Beat the bushes. Come up with *something.*"

A nose count of the persons known to have been in Craig around the time of the murders confirmed police suspicions that the killer must have arrived in Craig shortly before the slayings—say within a day or so—and left immediately afterward—say within an hour or so. Yet no one had seen him leave.

"That son of a bitch is still *here, amongst us,*" could be heard fairly often where fishermen and townspeople gathered on the streets and in the cafés and bars where the conversations inevitably turned to *him.*

"He could be any of us. He could be you, there, Morris."

"What ya talkin' about, man? You *don't* know what ya talkin' about. You better be careful accusing people, even if ya are jokin'. This is *serious.* The guy must be crazy mean to do something like this."

* * *

79

More and more it looked as though the death toll included the entire crew and that none had escaped, either as victim or suspect. Teams of detectives scouring Washington, delving into crew backgrounds, reported their results to Lieutenant Shover.

Dean Moon, who had fished several seasons with Coulthurst, apparently had idolized Mark.

"Dean thought of Mark as being sort of a father, a father figure," went the transcript of one interview with a close friend of Moon's. "And Mark treated him like a son. You can't be together for months at a time in the confines of a boat without establishing a close relationship."

Shover thought of *Mutiny on the Bounty,* during which close confinement resulted in an opposite sort of relationship.

The Alaskan adventure had been Jerome Keown's first with Coulthurst; it was learned that the honor student had been excited about it. It offered him a way of earning money to continue his studies. Keown simply wasn't, by any dark stretch of the imagination, killer material.

Neither was Chris Heyman. He telephoned home that Sunday before the *Investor* was seen leaving port on Monday morning.

"Fishing is *great!*" he told his mom. He babbled with exuberance. "Mark and all the guys are great guys. It's hard work, but I'm having a really good time."

Detectives pursuing the investigation in the lower 48 dispatched photos of Moon, Keown, and Heyman to Shover's men in Craig. Witnesses studied the photos and vowed with fair certainty that none of them was the youth they saw in the skiff. That meant they were probably dead.

And their killer still stalked the Northland.

As for Mark Coulthurst, investigators were unable to uncover a single harsh word against the big man. He simply had no enemies.

"Any man who ever fished with Mark would have jumped at a chance of going out as crew on his new boat," said another fisherman who had known the dead man since Mark wasn't much more than a teenager himself. "He liked taking the younger fellows with him because it gave them a chance to make money and continue with their educations. His crews were mostly college kids. He might have made bigger catches with more experienced crew, but that's the way Mark was."

Evidence thus far indicated a single killer——probably the guy from the skiff. But nothing indicated who he was or why he had, in apparent cold blood, gunned down eight people, including two little kids, and burned an $800,000 fishing vessel in an attempt to cover his crime.

The secret, Lieutenant Shover felt, lay somewhere between Saturday, September 4, when *Investor* came in for the weekend to celebrate the captain's birthday, and Monday morning, September 6, when the vessel was seen slowly steaming from her berth with a single shadowy figure at the helm. She burned off Egg Island the next afternoon.

The Coulthurst family and two crew members——no witnesses could agree upon exactly which two——were last seen Sunday night leaving a restaurant to return to the boat. The other two crewmen were already aboard. What had happened that Sunday night when the Coulthurst family returned?

What was the motive? That was the real puzzler. What drove a beast to murder six adults——presumably all six were killed, none escaping——and two children and leave them in a funeral pyre aboard their boat?

Two immediate motives came to mind. One was as old as human kind——greed. The other was more or less a product of modern society——drugs. But, of course, greed is what drugs are all about.

Not all the fishing boats in southeastern Alaska were chasing salmon. Some boats met mother ships that steamed under the cover of darkness into the Gulf of Alaska to unload contraband narcotics picked up in the Orient for distribution in the United States. The fishing boats received the drugs and stuffed them into the open bellies of salmon. The frozen salmon made their way then to Seattle and soon up the noses and into the veins of abusers from Los Angeles to New York.

"Not Mark Coulthurst!" went the immediate protest.

Okay, okay. Had he or his crew seen something suspicious—drugs being smuggled in? Did they know something they shouldn't have known, which could have resulted in the wiping out of possible witnesses?

It was one theory. It was no less plausible than the other motive—greed through robbery.

Even though *Investor* had been having a good season, it was well known that Coulthurst, like most captains, kept little if no cash aboard his boat. Payment for his catches was kept "on the books" at the cold-storage plant where he delivered his fish. Even the purchase of supplies like fuel, food, and other essentials was made "on the book," to be settled at the end of the season. Skippers even kept their seamen "on the book" until fishing was over. The most Captain Coulthurst and his fishermen had on them Sunday night was pocket money.

News media were all over the story, worse than gulls screaming and squabbling and darting above the Craig fish cannery.

"I can truthfully say," Lieutenant Shover told them, "that right now we do not have the name of anyone as a suspect. In fact, we still don't even know what happened aboard the *Investor*."

Chapter

15

Among the most difficult types of investigations fire cops face involve those fires set for profit, generally in efforts to defraud insurance companies. In recent years, insurance companies have taken certain measures to reduce their injuries and take the profit out of the crime by denying payments and by taking more care in underwriting risks. The American Insurance Association and other organizations cooperate with authorities in investigating fires of suspicious or incendiary nature and in pressing legislatures for more severe penalties for suspects convicted of arson. The Arson Reporting Immunity Law, adopted in some form by all 50 states, gives insurance companies immunity from lawsuits when sharing arson-related information with law-enforcement agencies. This means fire cops can gain access to insurance information without first obtaining a subpoena. Many states have gone a step further and instituted laws that permit law officers to in turn provide information to insurance companies.

When it comes to prosecuting offenders, district attorneys claim an abysmally poor record of success. On the other hand, insurance companies pursuing cases through civil courts checkmate fire starters at a much higher rate. The burden of proof in proving fraud as a civil offense is not nearly as severe as proving fraud and arson criminally. In civil court, there must only be a "preponderance of evidence" and agreement of two thirds of the jury; a criminal trial requires the defendant to be found guilty "beyond a reasonable doubt" and by the unanimous agreement of the jury.

New York Fire Marshal James McSwigin collected blatant evidence, including over a dozen witnesses, that two men connected with organized crime had conspired to torch a business belonging to one of them in order to defraud the insurance company. The case was delayed for nearly 2 years before it ever came to trial. A jury found the defendants not guilty.

Surprised that two obviously guilty men could be acquitted, McSwigin learned that the finding stemmed not only from the delay and from the case's being tried by a particular judge, himself questionable in ethics and associations, but also from a troubling public attitude toward insurance companies. The fire marshal and an assistant district attorney (DA) questioned the jurors about their verdict.

"Oh, Fire Marshal, there was no doubt the owner made the fire," said one juror. "We all agreed on that."

McSwigin blinked, stunned. "Then why wasn't he convicted?"

"Well, you did such a good job proving how he had spent so much money on cars and how he was so deeply in the hole that we felt sorry for him."

To which another juror chimed in, "Listen. Really, the only one affected by this is the insurance company. Nobody was hurt."

McSwigin felt a flush of anger. "What about the firefighters who risked their lives putting it out? How about the higher insurance premiums we all have to pay because of bogus claims?"

The two suspects, acquitted by criminal court, sued

in civil court for insurance payment of their $150,000 claim. Rules of evidence are less stringent in civil court; the fire marshal would have been allowed to say many things that he was not free to say during the criminal trial. The plaintiffs settled out of court for $18,000, giving them a huge personal loss in the burning of the service station.

Swindles take on many forms. During the administrations of Presidents Lyndon B. Johnson and Jimmy Carter, when low- and no-interest loans were available to rehabilitate tenement buildings, unscrupulous landlords and insurance agents worked up a most profitable scheme.

Typically, fire was set on the top floor of a vacant apartment building so that the roof would be sure to burn. Insurance pays maximum benefits only when the roof of the building is gone. Additionally, water pumped onto the top floor maximizes damage on lower floors, forcing tenants to move out when nothing else would. Rents were limited under rent-control laws.

With the building vacant, the landlord applied for federal loans to rehabilitate. He or she replaced the roof and made a few minor repairs, then insured it again.

Another fire. This time the tenement would burn to the ground. Once again, the landlord collected insurance. He also had the federal loan money in hand. Claiming he had no tenants, he would not pay back the federal loan. It was a form of double-dipping.

Because of the enormous profits associated with arson fraud, the thrust of BATF arson investigations is directed toward arson-for-profit schemes involving organized crime or white-collar criminals.

Chapter

16

Miami, Florida

The owner of the IWDC warehouse, Rami Rabjami, arrived at Bill Hamilton's BATF office for interrogation sipping hot ginseng tea. He was a small man with dark skin and signs of approaching age more in his hands than in his face, which otherwise remained remarkably untouched by his half century of life. He looked as collected and implacable as a neutered house cat when Hamilton ensconced him in the interview room.

Interrogating the owner of a torched business is an important step in an investigation. Experience teaches fire cops that all too frequently a lit match and an insurance claim prove enticing for an owner with an inventory of surplus merchandise or a seasonal inventory that has not moved, an owner who needs to dispose of property quickly to get out from underneath an oppressive mortgage, or one having marital problems or who needs money for hospital or medical bills or attorney fees.

Detective Wil Fuhrman conducted the interrogation. While his partners, Hamilton and McAllister, might be experts at a fire scene, it was the taciturn and methodical Fuhrman whose skills surfaced when it came to human evidence. Interrogation is both an art and a science that requires the skilled practitioner to know quite a bit about psychology, sociology, human behavior, and the motivations behind behavior.

Questioning accomplishes four things, broadly. First, it forces the subject to lay out a groundwork story by which known facts can be weighed. Second, it provides a measurement by which to compare future evidence and developments. Third, it nails down a potential suspect's alibi to prevent him or her from changing it as the case progresses and new evidence develops. Fourth, it furnishes the interrogator the opportunity to judge the subject and his or her veracity—or lack of it.

It is generally too high an expectation to hope the subject might confess guilt early in a probe.

Fuhrman sighed, drained the last of his coffee from a Styrofoam cup, crushed the cup in his fist, and slam-dunked it into a trash can. He trudged to the door of the interrogation room and entered the small, nearly bare cubicle where Rami Rabjami calmly sat sipping his brew.

"I will be happy to answer all your questions," Rabjami declared in his slightly stilted English. He oozed cooperation. "Has it been that you suppose some evil person has set aflame my warehouse?"

Fuhrman wasn't much for small talk in establishing rapport. He had a way of throwing people off-balance with his direct no-nonsense approach. "That's what we're here to determine," he replied gruffly. "Mr. Rabjami, are you insured for your losses?"

Rabjami didn't even blink. "Certainly I'm insured. But not nearly for a loss such as this. This is a complete and total disaster. Although most of our customers have their own insurance, I would suppose, I am personally responsible for the losses of those who do not."

Reflectively sipping his tea, the little man explained

something about his business, with little urging from the policeman. The warehouse, he said, regularly enjoyed between 20 and 30 clients who either stored excess merchandise or, since the warehouse was custom-bonded, cargo awaiting inspection by U.S. Customs. The majority of those customers were regulars. He had no new customers the month before the fire.

"Did any of your customers have significant insured losses?" Fuhrman asked.

"I believe them all to be honest people, if that is what you are asking. I have heard not even a rumor of any of them being associated with anything questionable."

"Have you fired any employees lately? Do you know of anyone with a grudge against you?"

"Grudge?"

"Hard feelings?"

"No one at all," Rabjami answered politely. "My business is family-owned and -run. Those few persons I employ outside the family have been with me for a very long time. None of them was materially invested. They will suffer as a result of this tragedy. They will no longer have jobs and my family will not have a business. We are destroyed."

The little owner's responses were precise. He said none of his employees reported seeing anyone suspicious hanging around the warehouse during recent weeks. Several customers delivered goods during the week of the fire and several others transferred merchandise out, which was not unusual activity. None of his employees used two-way radios.

He promised to provide investigators with a list of employees and relatives working for him currently or who had worked for him in the past and of everyone who had keys to the warehouse or who might have had them in recent months. He also promised a directory of customers and a schematic outline of where these customers' merchandise was stored in the warehouse.

"Were you warehousing any hazardous materials?"

Fuhrman probed. "Fertilizers, chemicals, gasoline, oil, acetone . . . ?"

Rabjami hesitated a heartbeat before shaking his head. "Only the few drums of insecticide. I don't recall anything else being declared. I did not want such things on hand. The records, bills, insurance policies, and other paperwork is being delivered to Mr. Hamilton's auditors."

". . . Paint thinner, petroleum ether, benzine, kerosene . . . ?" Fuhrman continued.

Rabjami shook his head.

"You would know if it were there?" Fuhrman asked.

"Naturally. It is my business."

"It *was* your business, Mr. Rabjami. Are you familiar with the uses of acetone?"

The detective watched his victim's expression carefully for flitting shadows of doubt or fear or guilt. Nothing.

"I'm not certain . . ." Rabjami faltered.

"Did you know it's used for processing cocaine?"

"How is it used?" Rabjami inquired, looking genuinely curious.

"Anything?" Hamilton asked eagerly when Fuhrman emerged from the interrogation.

"He knew of no hazardous materials kept in the warehouse."

"Right! So our torch simply backed up a truck and delivered 1,200 gallons of acetone through locked doors and set the place afire?"

"The man's either the world's greatest liar—outside Bill Clinton—or he had nothing to do with it."

Then, if not Rabjami, who benefited by the fire?

Cui bono?

Chapter

17

Craig, Alaska

Lieutenant Shover and his troopers on Prince of Wales Island had their own problems answering *cui bono?* in the murders of the crew aboard *Investor.* In the weeks following the discovery of the flames on the water, detectives uncovered on additional witness—a marina attendant who recalled a youth in a baseball cap purchasing 5 gallons of gasoline on Tuesday about noon, the day of the fire. He trudged off on foot with the gasoline in two separate containers. The attendant did not notice if he was coxswaining a skiff, if he was on foot, or what.

After that, everything was pure conjecture as to what happened aboard the trawler, why it happened, and who benefited enough to commit such a crime. Shover had his own theory based upon the known fact that the Coulthurst family went ashore Sunday evening to celebrate Mark's birthday, accompanied by two of the crew, while the other two seamen remained aboard ship.

A confrontation of some sort must have developed on *Investor* while the captain and his family were celebrating in Craig. The confrontation exploded into murder. The first two crewmen were killed in their quarters belowdecks. The killer was still there when the other two crewmen returned; he likewise killed them. Then he finished the job of eliminating all possible witnesses by wiping out the four Coulthursts.

The reason crew members aboard the *Decade*, to which *Investor* was warped, had not heard the gunfire was because skippers habitually kept generators running to supply current for their lights and refrigerators. The muffled but continuous thrumming of generators aboard both boats would have blanketed the sounds of gunshots.

The killer sailed *Investor* to Egg Island with the intent to destroy it. Only, unable to find anything flammable aboard, he had had to return in the skiff to purchase gasoline. That was when witnesses spotted him.

He had since disappeared, still unidentified.

The theory sounded as plausible as any other, although it still provided no answers to the questions of who and why.

"We have two persons—Mark and Irene Coulthurst—who were obviously shot and a bunch of other bodies that we cannot identify," Shover briefed his officers and newshounds pressing for a progress report. "When all you've got left is bones, you can't tell how they were killed. At least one of the bodies, that of the little boy, was totally consumed.

"We've got the remains of what might have been a gun, but it's just a hunk of metal. We've sent it to the FBI and it's possible they may be able to identify it as having been a rifle, but there is no way we can even determine that it might have fired the shots."

"Will you be able to solve this case?" a reporter demanded.

Shover stared at him a moment, frustrated. *How the hell should I know?* was what he wanted to say. Instead, he stalked out of the room and stood in the middle of

Craig's main drag and gazed off across the harbor toward Egg Island. The mound of the island sticking up above the cold blue-gray sea did resemble an egg. A chill breeze from the north ruffled his coat collar. Winter was coming, salmon season was over, and the little fishing village was dropping population fast as it settled in for first freeze.

The killer could be anywhere in the world by now.

The trooper took some solace in remembering another case in which a kid was murdered on the night he graduated from high school. It took 9 years to solve the case—but it *was* solved.

Chapter

18

Miami, Florida

It's known as following the paper trail. BATF auditors and paper shufflers painstakingly examined the business files of the IWDC turned over to them by Rami Rabjami while Hamilton, Fuhrman, and McAllister checked manifests against the debris and questioned owners of cargo stored in the warehouse.

"So far," Fuhrman growled, "nobody's claiming a loss of $20 million in delicate Egyptian artifacts."

Fire detectives learned that a company called Carib Tech Traders, Inc. rented warehouse space in the area where most of the CanChem jugs were recovered. Manifests listed stored items there as being audiovisual equipment with "deluxe" cabinets. Lab analysis confirmed that this particular area had been especially soaked with acetone. Of course, that could be mere coincidence, explained by the fact that the arsonist simply started fire in the most convenient place near an escape exit. It could even have been planned to divert suspicion from the true benefactor of the arson.

Using flashlights, Hamilton and McAllister poked and rummaged around in the warehouse near the center where the fire originated, like mice in a feed storage bin. HazMat and forensics had identified and separated what remained of storage, returning debris to roughly where it was before the blaze.

"What do you see?" Hamilton quizzed.

"What's left of some kind of cabinets."

"Do you see tubes, wires, microchips, relayers, circuit panels . . . ?"

"Only wooden stereo cabinets or something."

Hamilton nodded thoughtfully as Fuhrman joined the team.

"Carib Tech Traders is licensed in Florida to do business in exports and imports from the Far East," Hamilton explained to his partners. "The corporate officers are listed as Nayat and Najua Yordi—"

McAllister frowned, concentrating.

"Something ding your chimes on that one?" Fuhrman asked. "Or is it constipation?"

"I *know* that name," McAllister replied. "It's unusual enough that I'd remember it. Yordi. *Yordi.*"

"Do you want to hear a coincidence that I find interesting?" Hamilton went on. "Would it surprise you to learn that Rami and the Yordis are fellow Pakistanis?"

"Do I look surprised?" Fuhrman said dryly.

"Drug trade?" McAllister wondered.

Hamilton shrugged. "There are no police records on any of them. That's what makes it so damned perplexing. They seem to be clean, honest businesspeople."

"Money corrupts," McAllister said. "Enough money corrupts completely."

Using the Arson Reporting Immunity Law to access information about Carib Tech Traders and the other IWDC clients, detectives found out that Carib obtained a loan of $8,780.75 from a south Miami finance company the previous December, 9 months earlier, to pay premiums on a fire insurance policy of $600,000 on goods stored in the warehouse. On September 1, 2 days before the fire and nearly 3 months before the premium's renewal date, the Yordis again borrowed money to continue the $600,000 insurance policy.

Apparently, Carib Tech was not doing well as a business. It had several bank accounts scattered around Miami, the balance for none of which exceeded $5,000. The company was also paying off the borrowed insurance loans in small monthly payments.

In late July, Baronsgear Industries Ltd. of Taiwan had shipped audiovisual cabinets and radios to Carib Tech Traders in Miami. The Yordis paid Custom Clearance Dispatch of Miami $298 for that company's service in receiving the shipment and directing the cargo to IWDC for storage. The stored freight was listed with the insurance company as having a value of nearly a half-million dollars—$417,000. The entire cargo had apparently gone up in flames when fire destroyed Rabjami's warehouse.

It seemed to be all perfectly legitimate business—and not altogether *that* suspicious. After all, the insurance policy had been in effect for nearly a year. It wasn't like the Yordis suddenly went out the previous week and purchased a bucketful of insurance in anticipation of a fire. Thus far, they had made no insurance claims.

Nayat Yordi, about 50, and her 23-year-old unmarried daughter, Najua, lived in a typical sun-washed bungalow in a lower-middle-class neighborhood in northwest Miami, complete with garages and PTA meetings and bicycles left on narrow front lawns. Hamilton and Fuhrman parked their car in front of it. A tiny woman with a dark-featured face and furrowed brow answered their knock at her door. She resembled a flat-faced Pekingese pup and spoke in hesitant but correct English.

"May I help you, please?"

Fuhrman badged her. She stared uncomprehendingly.

"What is this about, please?"

"May we come in?" Hamilton asked. "We need to ask some questions. It's about the fire."

"Can you come back, please? We are only women and, you see, we are women alone since my husband died. We are not very good in business. We do not have the business head."

The detectives exchanged looks. All documents pertaining to the business—corporation papers, loans, checks—were signed either by Nayat or her daughter. That didn't seem to fit the image of helpless women.

"Just a few questions," Hamilton insisted.

The inside of the house appeared neat and well kept. Oriental tapestries and other artwork adorned the walls. A pair of men's jeans lay crumpled over a rocking chair. A younger version of the older woman came out of hiding, like a mouse from its hole, snatched the jeans, and disappeared.

"My daughter Najua," Nayat explained.

"Shy," Fuhrman said.

"It is her way, please."

"Could you ask her to come in also?" Hamilton requested.

The two women perched primly on the edge of a sofa while the detectives attempted to question them.

"We are merely, as you say, figureheads," Nayat said. "My son Afif and my sister's son, Kamal, are true heads of the family business now that my poor husband . . . now that he has gone."

It took Hamilton and Fuhrman only a short time to realize they were getting nowhere. The older woman and her taciturn daughter seemed more ignorant than evasive about the corporation and its activities and dealings. They bowed gracefully in demure, timid little half bows while they remained seated, the mother responding repeatedly with, "You must please ask my son and his cousin."

"We intend to," Fuhrman rumbled impatiently, "but it is you and your daughter who sign all the checks and papers."

"We are only figureheads, please, who are able to sign our names."

Hamilton gave up. "When can we talk to Afif and his cousin? What is his cousin's name again?"

"It is Kamal Jurdi, please. They are both away on business."

"A lot of that going around," Fuhrman grumbled. "Where are they? Colombia?"

"Away on business, please. They are often away and we do not always know where they are at a particular time."

Distilling information from this maddeningly polite pair was like trying to extract heat from a block of ice. The only emotional response elicited from the women occurred when Fuhrman pressured them about the whereabouts of Afif and Kamal. Tears welled in Nayat's eyes. She batted them away, then admitted reluctantly that her son seemed to have *disappeared.*

"Was it on Saturday we last saw him?" she asked her daughter.

"On Saturday after the fire?" Hamilton was quick to ask.

"Perhaps. I do not recall, please."

"Have you filed a missing-person report with the police?" Fuhrman asked.

"No, sir."

"Why not?"

"Because, please, I know my son will return."

As the fire cops departed in frustration, Fuhrman mused aloud. "Odd that Carib Tech still hasn't made a claim on the $600,000 in insurance money. You would have expected them to be camped out on the insurance company's front door. The other businesses with losses are."

"They're playing it cool," Hamilton suggested.

"Or Afif burned to death and is dumped in the Everglades."

"Or they're innocent—or the fire wasn't about insurance but about cocaine instead."

The or and if game could go on and on.

The IWDC arsonist's trail, paper or otherwise, virtually ended with the questioning of the Yordis, mother and daughter. Leads simply vanished, along with Afif Yordi and his cousin Kamal—not that they were necessarily viable suspects to begin with. The case turned into a waiting game as October leached away the last days of September and Halloween approached.

"At least," Rocky McAllister commented to Fuhrman, giving a kind of rationale for disappointment, "we're not in Detroit on Devil's Night."

Chapter

19

Detroit, Michigan

No one agreed on exactly when or how Devil's Night started, only that sometime in the mid-1980s cops and firefighters noticed that each year, on the night before All Hallow's Eve, an extraordinary number of fires were being ignited in the slum-ridden decay of southwest Detroit. There were 149 fires started in one four-square-block section of Delray in the heart of the slums. The news media soon picked up on the phenomenon and baptized the night before Halloween as Devil's Night. To cops, Devil's Night was another sign that the society was banging itself apart, like an engine that had run out of oil.

Set free and legitimized by the press, the spawn of hell emerged each year to unleash hellfire on Detroit. The city proved to be the ideal setting for such a lunatic practice. Slums surrounding the inner city were dark and forbidding, almost a separate city of filth and pollution populated by those down on their luck and the dregs of humanity blown about like wastepaper in the streets. The only places open nights were Coney Island hot dog shops and certain street corners and abandoned buildings where crack cocaine pushers and pimps plied their own devil's trade. Gotham City in the Batman movies could have been patterned after Detroit—except Detroit was so much darker.

Halloween in Detroit became synonymous not with ghosts and goblins but with flames and CHUDs—cannibalistic humanoid underground dwellers, so named from an old science-fiction movie. It became an insane night for firefighters, police officers, and arson cops as CHUDs went crazy and charged through city streets setting afire anything that would burn. Arson was the night's primary form of entertainment for the sick and twisted.

Fire cast a surrealistic glow over the inner city as CHUDs came out of hiding, like evil roaches, and scampered in the streets, chortling with glee and excitement and calling out to each other, backdropped by flames. Normally, CHUDs ignited garbage cans, Dumpsters and recycling receptacles, and abandoned buildings. In Delray, however, there was so much trash and garbage and the buildings were so stacked on top of one other, like part of the rubbish, that small fires readily exploded into large ones.

Sociologists attributed Devil's Night to poverty, neglect, and all the other social ills commonly blamed for everything. As for fire cops, they couldn't give a damn about what *caused* the dysfunction; they had their hands full catching CHUDs and preventing them from turning the city and its population into ashes and Crispy Critters.

Fire sleuth Lieutenant Colm "Scotty" Prentice, Detroit Fire Department, dreaded Devil's Night and resented the anarchy of the CHUDs. As his nickname implied, he was of Scottish lineage, with a ruddy face and the build of a muscular leprechaun. He had been with the fire department for more than 25 years and had worked every Devil's Night since the beginning. No Detroit firefighter received the night off when the

Devil ran amok. With the passage of the years, Devil's Night and its celebrants had grown increasingly vicious and careless of lives.

Scotty pulled his city sedan up in front of a blazing apartment building in Delray where firefighters battled desperately against their archenemy. Police held back an excited crowd part fearful and part jubilant. A chunky woman wearing a nurse's uniform seemed about to go into orbit as she threw herself around among the spectators, her shrieking inquiries providing jarring counterpoint to the roaring of the flames.

"Oh, God! Has anybody seen my baby? My little daughter! She's only three years old!"

Scotty grabbed her by the shoulders and spun her around. Her fingers clawed into his arms. She couldn't stop screaming. *My baby! My baby!"*

He shook her hard. "Calm down. Tell me about it."

"My little girl! She might still be in there alone. Maybe my son left her. He's a teenager."

Probably one of the CHUDs, Prentice thought with the cynicism of his breed, but he said, "Listen. What is the number of your apartment?"

"It's . . . it's upstairs . . . room . . . it's 215."

A mob of children and adults who escaped the fire was gathered around three fire rescue vehicles. Apparently, the little girl was not among the other survivors. The woman said she had checked. No one had seen her baby.

"You wait here," Scotty ordered. "If she's in there, we'll find her for you."

After jerking on turnouts, boots, and fire helmet, Prentice found the fire command officer (FCO) and told him about the little girl. The FCO nodded and ordered a patrol of three fighters to accompany the arson investigator into the inferno. None hesitated. Although no one was certain the little girl was trapped inside, even that small chance could not be ignored.

The initial entry assault against the front door met

defeat. Even the 2½-incher shooting a hard bolt of water the size of a fence post failed to lay the flames. Scotty called for a withdrawal. The blaze hissed and taunted and lapped insultingly around doors and windows.

"Scotty!" the FCO shouted. "We may have found a way. The alley."

Ladder crews counterattacking from the rooftop of an adjacent building and a hose company in the alley itself had fought flames clear from that side of the two-story apartment building. Smoke filled the alley and fighters continued soaking the exposure with water; the cold water felt good after the intense heat of the first assault.

A steel fire escape laddered up the side of the building to a second-floor door. Using the ladder meant entering the fire without a hose. Venturing into the interior without a line was a little like trying to navigate a typhoon at sea without a rudder. The hose was a fighter's protection and lifeline. Even experienced firefighters had been known to get lost without a hose to guide them, perishing within a smoke-filled room.

But it had to be done. Speed was vital.

"It's still hot as hell in there," a hose man warned.

Scotty replied with a lopsided grin. The night *was,* after all, Devil's Night.

The metal door at the top of the escape was either locked from the inside or jammed. Scotty gave up on it and used his fire ax to break through the window next to it. Smoke gushed through the fresh opening, but there were no flames mixed with it.

After the hose crew below prepped the room beyond with water, Scotty nodded to his Darth Vader–looka-like patrol—*Ready!*—and dived through the window into the darkened room beyond, followed by the three other fighters. They encountered dense smoke and violent heat. The floor felt like a hot griddle.

Testing the floor for stability one step at a time,

probing with laserlike beams from their flashlights, the rescuers gloved their way around the walls of the room to a door. The door opened into a narrow hallway so filled with smoke it was like entering a dark cave. There was a dim fire glow somewhere ahead.

It wasn't enough that they got *inside* the building; they also had to get *out*. Scotty made mental note of distances and landmarks—five steps to a fire extinguisher on the wall, three more to an old chair left in the hallway—as he pushed into the building's smoky bowels. A half century of slow dry-rotting had left many of the tenements in Delray warped and unstable. Fire eating out what remained of the building's support caused the landing to creak and vibrate beneath the firefighters' heavy footfalls. Scotty carefully tested each step before trusting his weight to it. He checked the numbers on the hallway doors by using his flashlight and pressing his glass-shielded face next to them—*212 . . . 214 . . .*

"Here it is!" he announced.

The door to 215 was unlocked. Heat, smoke, and darkness extended from the hallway into the apartment. Even wearing heavy boots, the firemen hopped from foot to foot to keep from scorching their feet. They blundered into furnishings and tripped over toys and other things left on the floor as they worked their way along the walls. A thin tongue of flame flickered through the floor to one side, very near. Fire was chewing the floor out from underneath them.

Hurry! Scotty heard—telepathically, it seemed—the exhortation from the others. *Hurry!*

Adults trapped inside a blazing structure often retained enough presence of mind to work their way to windows where rescue workers on ladders might pluck them to safety. In contrast, children, the ill, and the senile frequently succumbed to panic and tried to hide from fire—under beds, inside closets, in the bathtub . . .

Driven by the urgency of the situation, Scotty and his men fought their way in agonizing slow motion from room to room, searching hiding places where a small girl might conceal herself. Flashlight beams finally picked her out bundled in a small mound beneath covers on her bed. Scotty took two steps and scooped up the still form in his arms.

The body dissolved into a pillow and a bundle of blankets. There was no one inside the apartment. The child wasn't here.

The floor crackling beneath, trembling and sighing as though about to heave up its guts, reminded the rescuers that time had run out. They made one last quick exploration with their flashlights and, by unanimous consent, headed for the hallway. There was no time left to search the other apartments. Scotty felt sick at his stomach at their failure, but they simply could stay no longer without perishing themselves.

Theirs was no retreat from the cauldron of flames; it was a rout. With the floor shaking and vibrating, flames hissing and slithering like serpents, the firefighters bolted into the hallway and hurried toward the escape ladder, Scotty counting off the landmarks as they passed them. The floor directly behind seemed to emit a dying sigh of resignation as they reached the open door of the apartment through which they had entered the building. The last fighter in line paused to take a look, like Lot's wife turning to take her last peek at Gomorrah.

Scotty seized him and hurled him through the doorway—just as the hallway collapsed with a jolting rumble and became the fiery mouth of an erupting volcano. One of the fighters slammed the door against the flames as though to keep out the bogeyman.

Pursued by searing heat and howling flames as the floor sagged like cloth beneath their feet, the firefighters scrambled out the window onto the fire escape. Hose companies below and on the next roof covered their retreat with columns of water. Scotty blistered his palms through his gloves sliding down the hand railings. None of them stopped running until they were out of the alley and in the street. The building sounded like it was finally dying.

Scotty threw off his SCBA mask and looked back. Flames throbbed through the roof and showered the night sky with sparks.

"The little girl?" a truckie said.

"She—she wasn't in the apartment," Scotty managed through his coughing.

"That's what I'm trying to tell you. Her brother took her to a friend's house down the block. Their mama's with them now."

Chapter

20

Detroit, Michigan

Devil's Night and CHUDs were truly a mating in hell. Worse yet, CHUDs were rarely arrested and even more infrequently brought to trial and convicted. There was seldom any evidence and almost never any witnesses, at least none willing to step forward. Arson investigator Scotty Prentice stewed about the Devil's Night arson that almost took his life and the lives of three other firefighters, not to mention the lives of apartment residents, but then he dismissed the incident as hopelessly insoluble—until one night a few days later. He happened to catch the evening news on TV.

To his surprise, this son of a bitch was *on television* confessing to the apartment-house fire and dozens of others he had set on previous Halloweens since he was 12 years old. As part of a special feature on arson, a local TV news team was interviewing arsonists themselves, true experts on the subject. Their interviewees were shown disguised in darkened silhouettes with their voices electronically deconstructed.

"I'll be damned," Scotty murmured, then telephoned his superior, Fire Marshal Bob Muhollak. "Switch to the news," he said.

"I'm watching it."

"Notice anything familiar about that creep? The broad nose, the way forehead and chin both recede away from the nose?"

"No . . . wait a minute. That's *Buddy Carlton.* That little sack of human garbage."

Fire cops had been trying to nail high-profile CHUD Buddy Carlton for years. Not that he *personally* started all the Devil's Night fires in Delray. Being civic minded and a neighborhood idol to the dysfunctional Delray teens, he had made it his pet project to instruct up-and-coming younger CHUDs in the art of combustion. What was the world coming to when *heroes* were little weak-chinned bastards who set people's houses ablaze?

Knowing Buddy was the arsonist confessing on TV and *proving* it were two separate things. Scotty went to the reporters and appealed to their sense of justice and community in an attempt to persuade them to testify against Carlton. Buddy had admitted on the air that he would be out again next year trying to burn Detroit down. Reporters being reporters, however, and devoid of any moral center, they hid behind the First Amendment and their right to keep their sources secret.

That was when Scotty approached Fire Marshal Muhollak with his own plan.

"Everyone has a chance for his fifteen minutes of fame," he said, chortling. "I propose to give Buddy a double dose of fame."

"It borders on illegal entrapment," the fire marshal argued.

"All we have to do is tape him confessing to his arsons the way he did on *real* TV," Scotty explained. "I think he'll confess legitimately after that."

"It's splitting legal hairs."

"Skipper, he could have killed a little girl this Devil's Night, and he damn near *did* murder firefighters in that apartment building. He'll be back next year unless we stop him."

What did they have to lose?

"I'm certain he'll give an Academy Award performance," Scotty said, grinning.

The scheme depended upon traits criminals possessed in abundance—arrogance and stupidity. All it required was a van with a phony TV logo and TV NEWS TEAM painted on its sides and a few firefighters pretending to be a camera crew. Because most of the CHUDs knew Scotty on sight, he had to settle for hiding inside the van while the "news team" cruised Delray interviewing people about Devil's Night.

Young fire starters enamored of cameras and the fame they offered literally fought for the opportunity to stand in front of the big eye and relate their fire adventures. The young arsonists' bragging and boasting made Scotty feel ill.

At first, Buddy Carlton seemed suspicious and remained in the background. He kept edging closer and closer. He simply could not stand *not* being the center of attention. After all, wasn't *he* the king of the CHUDs?

"I been on TV before," he finally ventured to say to the camera crew.

Scotty had coached the firemen to work on Buddy's ego. "Oh? On *Sesame Street?*" the firefighters in disguise chided, then pointedly ignored Carlton and turned to another kid. "You there. Do you want to be next on camera?"

In his early twenties and therefore feeling deserving of precedence, Buddy pushed the younger boys aside.

"You could use me again," he suggested.

The firefighter-cameraman looked at him. "Why would we want to do that?"

"Shee-*it,* man. All these motherfuckers know who I be. I done set 'most every fire around here."

"I don't really have no reason," Buddy Carlton said in his subsequent confessions of having torched more than 100 structures. "I just likes to do it. It makes me feel good."

Scotty Prentice watched with a combination of frustration and fascination as psychiatrists and psychologist glued themselves to the case. The shrinks debated about why Buddy felt the need to destroy by fire and how *he* could best be served, best helped by the criminal justice system. Most of them suggested that panacea for all life's problems in modern America—counseling.

"It's one of the first crimes of true pyromania I've personally encountered," exclaimed one shrink. "The youngster is sexually aroused by setting fires. Amazing!"

What was most annoying, in Scotty's viewpoint, was how judges and lawyers and psychiatrists and politicians never seemed to understand what ordinary people saw as simple common sense—that the *first* duty of society was not to *help* the perpetrators of heinous crimes but to protect the population from their antisocial behavior.

"With Buddy in jail," cracked Charley Evangelo, Prentice's partner, "all we have to worry about are hookers and pimps, crackheads, thieves, and Buddy's minions left behind. That's what—about ninety-five percent of the city?"

As a final act of dumb defiance, Carlton showed up for his court hearing* wearing a Devil's Night T-shirt.

"I see you dressed for the occasion," Scotty commented.

---

*Buddy Carlton was eventually convicted of first-degree arson and sentenced to serve 10 years in the state penitentiary.

Chapter

21

In the world of fires and arson, Buddy Carltons are relatively uncommon. Experts estimate that economic gain takes the major share of the pie when it comes to arson—somewhere between 40% and 50%. Rarely does the insurance policy beneficiary set his or her own fires. Commonly, he will hire a "torch" to do it while he or she establishes an alibi, preferably placing the beneficiary somewhere out of town or out of state. One New York City slumlord paid to have 26 of his own buildings burned in order to collect the insurance money.

Arson rings, more and more frequently composed of members of organized-crime families, have formed in most large cities to specialize in insurance fires. The leader of a ring can be almost anyone—a housewife in Des Moines, an attorney in Los Angeles, an insurance claims adjustor, a judge, a cop. The typical ring may consist of the leader, an intermediary who makes contact with clients to protect the leader, and one or more torches who can be called upon to do a job. However, sometimes torches and an assistant may comprise the entire ring.

FIRE COPS

One arson scam involved 13 members of a single family. Two or three of them would move into a new town, rent a small house in the suburbs or in a rural area, buy new furniture on credit, and obtain insurance on the entire lot. After a short while, the new furniture would be removed and junk would be substituted. Then there would be a fire. Once the gang collected insurance money, it moved on to a new town.

A New York City judge was found guilty of operating a real-estate business through a pattern of racketeering crimes including extortion, arson, and mail fraud. Because of rent control, he was unable to either raise rent on low-paying or elderly tenants or evict them without cause. Therefore, he began a campaign of harassment and deception by filing fraudulent eviction proceedings and having torches burn and vandalize premises to drive out unwanted renters.

In Washington State, seven defendants of a group known as the Family pleaded guilty to racketeering involving at least 10 arsons and numerous mail-fraud schemes.

Eleven Chicago racketeers were found guilty in a RICO (Racketeer Influenced and Corrupt Organizations) case involving a Greek organized-crime syndicate specializing in extortion and arson.

Boston arson investigators spent 4 months examining 150 suspicious fires in which three people died and more than $6 million was paid in insurance claims before they uncovered a gang of 33 members composed of wealthy landlords, real-estate operators, attorneys, a former arson squad captain, and a former member of the state fire marshal's office. Some members of the ring sold burned tenements, from which insurance monies had already been collected, to other members at ridiculously low prices. The new owner would then notify an insurance company that he planned to rehabilitate the structure and take out builder's insurance. Shortly after the new policy took effect, another fire would break out.

In south Florida, word in the criminal underworld had it that Carl Elwes charged a flat 10% of loss to torch your business for you, guaranteed to make it look accidental or your money cheerfully refunded.

Chapter

22

Miami, Florida

When Lou Ciccarola first bought the Diamond Bar on one of the main drags 6 years earlier, he called it the Diamond Bar & Grill. It was different from the usual Miami tourist joints specializing in frozen "tropical" drinks and pictures on the walls of local fishing tournaments. He had a fat cook who whipped up a grease burger or an even greasier burrito in 2 minutes flat. Working stiffs from the neighborhood kept the trade brisk and regular, which was supplemented by snowbird winter vacationers from the trailer parks and kids coming in to eat, play pool, and do some underage beer drinking.

"I wanted a place I could feel at home in and where the folks who came in could feel the same way," Lou explained to his best friend Bernie. "It didn't necessarily have to be a place where everybody who walked in off the street knew your name. I wanted it to be where no one gave a shit if they knew your name or not."

Business started going downhill 4 years later after the cook got drunk and thrown in jail, then migrated north.

Lou knocked off the *& Grill* from his sign. At the end of the year, after figuring expenses, he discovered the Diamond had lost more than its luster. It was losing money.

He blamed it on Sheridan's Bar, which had opened two blocks away. Sheridan's was brighter and more upbeat than the Diamond. It offered specials on beer and bar drinks every night until 10 P.M., served by sexy waitresses. Co-op–owned, it could afford to lose a few bucks until it ran its privately owned competitor out of business. Lou felt himself going under.

He was complaining about it one night to his best friend Bernie over beers in the Diamond. Leave it to Bernie to try to help. Bernie knew this guy, he said, who could take care of all Lou's problems.

"How?" Lou asked, interested.

It was after hours and there was no one else in the bar, but Bernie leaned conspiratorially across the table.

"What if Sheridan's was to burn down?" he asked. "Would you call that luck or what?"

"I'd call it the luckiest day of my life."

"I know this guy who can help luck along a little."

Lou straightened up and stared. "I don't know, Bernie . . ."

Bernie threw up his hands. "Hey, I'm just telling you I know him. Using him is up to you."

That was the way it was left for a while. But the more Lou thought about it, the better he liked the idea. After all, he had to do *something* to prevent going belly up. It would be self-defense.

For the first time in months, he felt the stirrings of hope.

Bernie said he would make the arrangements. "My connection will stop by the Diamond one evening this week," he said. "He'll come in and ask, 'How's business?' That's your cue. Got it?"

" 'How's business?' "

"What you'll say back is 'Business sucks.' That's his cue to let him know you're both on the same wavelength, that you're each who you think the other is. He'll come back—he'll go, 'I have a few suggestions about how you can make it better.'"

Lou shook his head, frowning. "Why do we have to go through all this cloak-and-dagger nonsense? Why can't I give you the money and you arrange everything?"

"Can't do, bud. I'm on probation. But go along with the guy. He's a real professional. He'll take care of all your troubles."

"I don't want to be implicated."

"Lou. Lou. The guy is a *professional.*"

It was a long week for Lou, waiting for the connection to show up. It made him jumpy. He eyed each stranger, the few who came in anymore those hard-luck days.

On Friday, there were maybe eight or 10 people in the bar. It was about 9 P.M. on what should have been his busiest night of the week but wasn't anymore. Lou settled his considerable bulk on a stool to watch rerun episodes of the 1960s sitcom *I Dream of Jeannie* on the TV mounted on the wall between the men's and women's restrooms. He failed to notice the guy come in until he spoke.

"So, how's business, Lou?"

Lou almost jumped off his bar stool.

"Lou?"

The new guy wore a sly, twisted smile. He was a man of about 30 or so, with thinning blondish hair and the same chinless features as a possum. His hands and eyes never stopped moving, like a ferret's. To Lou, he looked gutter sneaky and bite-you-in-the-ass mean, the looks of a guy who wouldn't stand up face-to-face to you but instead got even in some other way. He would have been a barn burner a century earlier.

"So how's business?" he repeated.

Lou's tongue thickened. What was that response? "Uh . . . not so good." *Oh, shit!* "I mean . . ."

"I know what you mean, Lou." The guy kept wearing what Lou's old dead daddy would have called a "shit-eating dog's grin." He said, "Why don't you have a drink with an old friend, Lou? Maybe I have some suggestions about how to make business better. Lou, I am here to solve all your problems."

Before entering his present occupation, Carl Elwes had tried clerking at a convenience store and had swept out more than a few bars and restaurants and washed lots of dishes. Then he discovered how to make *real* money—easy money—the fun way, with fire. God, how he loved this job. He considered himself an artist at it.

The only thing he disliked about it was the shit-heads you had to work with. Take Big Larry, for example, who was so big and dumb that—Christ!— he had gone down to the state pen at Raiford *three* separate times. Larry was never going to be an artist in the business. He lacked imagination, passion, and drive. But he went along with whatever he was ordered to do, kept his mouth shut afterward, *and* worked cheaply. You had to take what you could get. It was difficult to find anybody competent to apprentice in this profession.

"Carl likes to brag, show how smart he is," said Larry, after his last job with Carl Elwes. Together, they had torched a little café, a house, a rich man's yacht, and then Sheridan's Bar. "I don't know what all he might have done on his own or with somebody else. He didn't talk about nothing he did. He was real secretive that way. He learned from when he got busted before that you don't never talk out of school. Know what I mean? We ain't buddies or nothing. When he had a job for me, he'd call and I'd meet him someplace. He'd already have the stuff to do it with. We'd go do it; then I wouldn't hear from him again until the next time."

Being a perfectionist and an artist, Carl scouted Sheridan's Bar for two nights in a row to figure out its patterns and layout. It fronted one of the main arteries into downtown Miami from the north. An alley behind it, however, offered convenience and concealment in approaching the back door. The lighting in the alley was poor and several cars had been junked in it. Employees and customers of the all-night International House of Pancakes down the street often parked their cars in the alley. Police would never notice an extra vehicle parked for a few minutes anywhere in the vicinity.

The bar manager was seldom on premises during regular working hours, but he always showed up at around 2 A.M. or so to count the night's take. He let the barmaids and the bartender leave, then locked up himself when a rent-a-cop came to escort him to the nearest drive-through bank. Sheridan's was finally abandoned after 3 A.M.

It was going to be a piece of cake. The locks on the back door were shitty and there were no electronic alarms. The manager apparently figured the bar's location facing a busy street was security enough. *Right!*

As instructed, Larry stole a license plate to put on Elwes's old blue Ford work van, just in case some nosy bastard spotted the vehicle hanging around and took down the number. Elwes played every angle, left nothing to chance. The fire starters arrived an hour early on the night Elwes selected to do the job. They parked on the road so Carl could observe the bar and make sure everyone left on time. Big Larry clambered into the back of the van and was soon sleeping like a hibernating bear. He smelled like one too. His snoring annoyed Carl.

Finally, Elwes reached across the backseat and shook Larry. "Wake up, asshole."

Larry snorted and hacked and farted. *Jesus God.*

"Come on, asshole. Get up. It's time. And stop spitting and farting in my fucking van, you pig."

"Carl, why do you call me asshole? I ain't no asshole."

"Some freaks think an asshole is the best part of a man."

"I ain't one of them. Is it time?"

"We have about an hour before daybreak. This is the quietest time of the night."

Carl whistled cheerfully as he pulled the van around the block and entered the alley, turning off the van's lights. He had removed the brake lights altogether. He hesitated behind the wheel for a minute, looking.

"Get the cans, asshole," he said.

He grabbed a knapsack and a crowbar while Big Larry hoisted a pair of heavy 5-gallon containers. They scurried to the back door of Sheridan's Bar. Larry always started getting nervous at this point.

"I need a cigarette bad," he complained. "To calm my nerves."

"Not now, you moron."

Elwes forced the edge of the crowbar between the facing and front of the door next to the lock. He retrieved a hammer from his knapsack and struck the end of the prybar a ringing blow. Two or three more hammer blows drove the crowbar deep. He leaned his weight hard against the bar, grunting. The door buckled slightly.

"Kick it," he commanded Larry.

The door flew in and opened, banging. The burglars ducked inside and closed the door. They found themselves inside the kitchen next to a walk-in freezer. Pale light from a Budweiser sign guided them along the short hallway to the barroom. Larry eased his heavy containers to the floor. Carl unscrewed the caps. A bitter wood smoke odor wafted through the building.

"All the pros use acetone," Elwes explained. "Very efficient."

After checking for pilot lights and other open flames and finding none, he took one of the jugs and motioned Larry to the other.

"Hurry. We don't have much time," he snapped. "Don't be shy with this shit. Start at the front and splash it evenly all over the place. Stay down out of sight when you're by the windows."

"Don't you think I know nothing, Carl?"

"Sure I do. You're a fucking genius."

They soaked everything, starting at the front door of the main bar and working back over the dining area and through the kitchen. Acetone was corrosive to the throat and windpipe, but it wasn't as bad as gasoline. Gasoline was for amateurs.

"This place'll go off like a firecracker," Carl said.

"It's starting to get daylight," Larry said nervously.

Elwes had experimented with different timers before he finally settled on the egg timer as the quickest, simplest, and least traceable method of ignition. He fished one from his bag.

"We'll set it in the front of the building so the first blast will light up the front," he explained. "If we started the fire at the back door, it would be too easy for the fire department to get inside through the front and take control. Our client wants this place taken out permanently."

Moron or not, Larry should recognize and appreciate the thought a real artist puts into his work.

"It's getting daylight, Carl. The cops'll see us."

"Why are you so fucking jittery? I know what I'm doing."

"It stinks in here."

Elwes rigged the egg timer to spark once the little buzzer sounded. He squatted near the front door, twisted the dial, and tapped the start button. The timer started clicking. Larry watched, standing back a few feet while he fidgeted and twisted his big hands. He patted his shirt pockets.

"We've got about three minutes," Elwes said, sounding satisfied with his work.

He rose to his feet and turned toward Larry.

His blood became ice.

Marlboro leaped out at him like a neon light and burned itself into his retinas. Larry's thick hands fumbled with a cigarette lighter.

"No!"

It was a while after the tremendous sudden light and heat that Carl Elwes opened his eyes. He squinted. He lay on his back and it was full daylight. Bright blue Florida sky surrounded him like a canopy. Tendrils of smoke etched up from Sheridan's Bar across the street. Fire engines and police cars were everywhere, their lights blipping. A man bent over him.

"Are you okay?" a voice asked.

"Do I look fucking okay to you?" Elwes croaked. He hardly recognized his own voice.

The man introduced himself as a cop, an arson investigator. "Stop me if you've heard this before," he recited. "You have the right to remain silent. Anything you say can and will be held against you—"

"Huh?" Elwes groaned. "Hospital . . ." he rasped. "Don't know what you're talking about. I was only walking by on the street—"

"Carrying ten gallons of *acetone?*"

"I wan' lawyer . . ."

Goddamned moron Larry. He really is an asshole. He just had to have his fucking cigarette. . . .

120

Also wrapped like a mummy, Big Larry ended up in a police-guarded hospital room down the hall from Elwes's.*

"Big *dumb* asshole Larry," Elwes muttered underneath his breath, his wrapped fingers forming claws as though closing around his former cohort's throat. "Don't give him any cigarettes," he implored nurses and detectives. (This was back when hospitals allowed patients to smoke.) "I want that bastard to *suffer.*"

---

*Carl Elwes and Larry were both convicted of arson and sentenced to relatively short terms in the Florida State Penitentiary. Lou Ciccarola was implicated but never convicted; his business flourished after the elimination of competition. Although acetone was used as an accelerant, investigators Hamilton, Fuhrman, and McAllister were unable to link Elwes to the IWDC fire.

Chapter

23

Sapulpa, Oklahoma

At least Mark Coulthurst, his family, and his crew aboard *Investor* in Craig, Alaska, were likely dead of gunshot wounds before their bodies were torched in an effort to cover up the crime. A young couple in Sapulpa, Oklahoma, a suburb of Tulsa, were not quite so fortunate. Sapulpa Police Sergeant Harley Hausam spotted the fire. It was a cool morning on October 6, just at dawn. The blaze, a single roaring little sun of a fireball in the middle of a vacant field on the northeastern outskirts of the little city, heralded its separate sunrise.

Sergeant Hausam radioed for the fire department and stood by in the field until a pumper arrived. An old Oldsmobile Cutlass that had seen its best days 20 years before sat blackening and scorching at the center of the fireball. Hausam might have assumed the car was stolen, except for its ancient vintage. Cars taken out for joyrides and then torched to destroy prints——it happened all the time. Normally, however, thieves preferred newer cars.

The fire department quickly doused the fiery wreck, except for flames snaking out of the trunk. Firefighters popped the compartment lid to get at the enemy. They recoiled in horror.

"They were cooked alive in the trunk," Tulsa Police Sergeant Steve Steele told reporters that afternoon when he joined the investigation. Steele, in his mid-thirties, was relatively young for a homicide detective. His blond good looks made him look even younger. "A man and a woman," he said, "burned almost beyond recognition."

The two corpses crammed into the trunk were charred and blackened. At the end, it seemed, they had sought comfort in one another, for the bodies were clasped in what remained of each other's arms. It was startlingly apparent that they had been *alive* when the fire was set. Steele's expression remained fixed, concealing the revulsion he already felt for the unknown perpetrator.

The ploughed field, readied for a crop of winter wheat, lay between Sapulpa and Tulsa. By good daylight, detectives, crime-scene specialists, and fire investigators were swarming over the crime scene searching for clues to the victims' identities and to that of the perpetrator of what the news media was already calling "one of the most heartless crimes in America." Detective Steve Steele from Tulsa joined investigator Bruce Duncan of the Sapulpa Police Department on the scene, both wearing coats against the October chill. Duncan was tall, maybe a few years older than Steele, with the characteristic slumping shoulders of people who carry with them firsthand knowledge of human foibles and crimes.

Knocking loose clues from the fire-ravaged vehicle and the surrounding landscape proved all but impossible. Fire had destroyed anything remotely useful as evidence. Duncan and Steele were left with only vague speculations as to what might have occurred and why. Their only lead proved to be the license plate number. At least it was a start to identifying the victims.

In most cities in Oklahoma, as in a number of other states, fire marshals are responsible for ensuring fire safety, handling code violations, and determining the origin and cause of suspicious fire. The investigation of crimes associated with the arson, especially murder, is assigned to police detectives, who themselves are trained in fire-related crimes. After fire marshals determined that the blaze had been ignited by someone cutting a fuel line to leak gasoline into the engine compartment, then striking a match to it, the case went to Steele and Duncan.

The investigation of a classic homicide case, if such existed, almost always began with the discovery of the body—in this instance, *two* bodies. First, the corpse in such cases is identified. Then detectives begin the painful process of tracking the last days and even hours of the victim's life in order to discover the point at which the victim encountered the killer. Somewhere along that pathway, they hope to pick up a telltale piece of evidence that delineates motive. Motive often produces a suspect.

Most of Tuesday found Duncan and Steele, either separately or together, backtracking step by step the tag number left on the burned hulk of the Oldsmobile. Steele found himself in the Tulsa home of the parents of a 22-year-old Oklahoma State University coed, Laura Lee Sanders. He couldn't be sure from the photo shown him if this young woman was the same as the one in the car trunk. The young woman in the photo was slender and dark-haired and had great, pretty eyes and a warm, open smile.

The Cutlass, however, was hers. And she had not come home from her evening shift the previous night at a restaurant on East 21st Street in Tulsa. Her father, fearful and distraught as only a father can be when notified by the police that one of his offspring might be dead, seemed to want to talk, as though talking postponed the agony of having to accept reality.

"She was a little frustrated. . . ." he said, rambling a little. "She didn't know what she wanted to get her degree in. She was taking some time off from college to think about it. She took the job as a waitress in the meantime."

He paused, swallowing. He had also been diagnosed as having cancer, he said. Laura Lee wanted to be near her father during this trying time.

"I—I never thought that . . . that *she* would . . ."

Steele dreaded such moments, speaking to the survivors of crime victims. Although he was a young man, he had seen too much death during more than a decade as a Tulsa police officer, the last several years as a homicide detective.

In the meantime, checking through the restaurant where Laura Lee had worked, Duncan, the tall detective from Sapulpa, was also having his encounters with a survivor. She was the wife of 27-year-old Michael William Houghton, the bartender at the restaurant. Houghton also had not come home from work last night. It was the first such time in the couple's three-year marriage.

Houghton was an athletic man who had been a high-school and college track star. When he was only in the sixth grade, a national comparison listed him as the eleventh fastest boy in the nation. He tended bar 3 nights a week, taught guitar for a music company, and played in a rock 'n' roll band while he prepared to attend law school after having earned a degree in political science from Tulsa University.

With this groundwork laid, Steele and Duncan soon learned that not only had Laura Lee and Houghton worked together, but they had been close friends for a number of years, even before Houghton's marriage. In fact, the two often went together somewhere to unwind nights after closing the restaurant. Houghton's wife knew of the friendship and did not disapprove.

"Mike is a real straight-ahead guy," a friend of

Houghton's assured Detective Duncan. "There was no hanky-panky going on between those two. They were just friends."

"My husband is not cheating on me," Mrs. Houghton insisted.

After closing time at the restaurant on Monday night, Laura Lee and Michael left in their separate vehicles—she in her old Cutlass, he in his 2-year-old dark blue Isuzu pickup truck bearing Oklahoma plate ZPB-626. There was an upscale trendy bar near 41st and South Peoria in the Brookside area where young people often gathered. Houghton and Sanders were last seen sitting together, talking, in Laura Lee's car in the alley parking lot at the bar at 1 A.M. Another young woman, a friend, had stopped by to chat with the couple a few minutes.

"They were fixing to go home," she told Duncan. "That wasn't anything out of the ordinary for them to be talking like that. They could talk to each other about anything."

The case bore the marks of a possible lovers' triangle. Yet somehow, neither Steele nor Duncan saw it that way. Laura Lee had no steady at the time, and Houghton's wife was simply not jealous of her husband's friend.

Okay. What was the answer?

By late that afternoon, dental records confirmed that the burned corpses in the Oldsmobile were indeed those of Laura Lee Sanders and Michael William Houghton. Autopsies revealed they died of fire and smoke inhalation. Neither had been seriously injured prior to death—except . . .

Except Laura Lee had been *raped*. Not simple sexual intercourse that might have occurred between two consenting adults, but rape—the brutal kind that bruised and tore internal tissue.

Laura Lee's car was burned; Michael's Isuzu pickup was missing. Gone. A nationwide alert went out requesting all occupants of the vehicle be held if it were apprehended.

"It looks like we're in a holding pattern right now," Sapulpa Assistant Police Chief Ron Sole said in briefing his department heads. "But if we can find that truck, we can get some real insight into what's going on here."

After only the first day, the case was like a ball of twine rolled tightly with no ends loose to provide a starting point for unraveling it. It remained that way for the following several days while Steele and Duncan and other sleuths kept up an exhausting schedule.

They pored over the names and descriptions of possible suspects; they studied criminal MOs (modus operandis); they cornered snitches; they used computer analysis to kick out details of similar crimes nationwide.

They pounded the streets asking questions; they pressured underworld thieves, sex offenders, and ex-convicts; they fanned out across Tulsa County in efforts to squeeze a drop of information out of someone, somewhere.

What evil lurked in a mind that would conceive of rape, of locking two people *alive* in a car trunk, cutting a fuel line, and then setting the car afire to cover up the original crime?

Chapter

24

Woodstock, New York

Evil terrifies most when it remains within the realm of the unknown. Evil associated with fire conjures up images of hell and the Devil. Yet evil, reprehensible and horrific when it has no face, when it remains in the shadowy dark, loses its power when it is brought into daylight and given a human face. Take, for example, the Woodstock arsons.

Over a period of 7 months, from May to November, farmers and gentlemen city farmers in Woodstock, 80 miles north of New York City and made famous by the 1969 rock festival, patrolled their yards by flashlight or kept anxious watch from their windows at night, fearful of a mystery arsonist burning down their barns—a barn burner reincarnated from those who once plagued New York and Boston during Colonial times, when such fire starters were hanged, burned at the stake, or at least banished.

The mystery torch incinerated 10 barns during those 7 months and attempted that many more, causing in excess of $1 million in damage. His MO was to place road flares into hay or whatever proved combustible inside, and then vanish. The mere mention of him brought shudders. He took on the aura of a specter, a surreal figure from another world somehow wreaking vengeance upon the town for some unnamed sin.

"I can't sleep," said one man. "I know my barn is next—but I don't know *why*. We're terrified he'll start on houses next."

"He's the bogeyman," exclaimed a child, and no one disagreed.

On the night of November 21, Heidi Motzkin glanced out her window and spotted the glow of a just-started fire in the Vincors' barn across the road. Her hand flew to her open mouth and she stumbled back in shock and disbelief. For skulking away from the barn in the darkness, his face momentarily aglow from the blaze just started, was a man virtually everyone in town knew and liked.

"I could hardly believe my eyes," Mrs. Motzkin exclaimed, when she notified the police and fire departments. "It was Vernon. Vernon's doing it!"

Vernon Shultis, 58, was a mild-mannered truck driver and a lifelong resident of Woodstock. His family had been in the area since the 1700s and had, in fact, owned much of the land upon which barns were now being burned. The extended Shultis family was no longer land rich, but the family name remained woven into the fabric of the town. Vernon had worked the last several decades with the highway department and had been a volunteer firefighter.

"Everyone is somehow connected here. It's almost incestuous in a certain sense," said Town Supervisor Tracy Kellogg.

After Shultis was arrested and indicted for the fires, crimes that, if he was convicted of them, could draw him 15 years in prison, fear and anger in the community gave way to something surprisingly different. The "bogeyman" turned out to be one of their own, not at all a scary stranger or otherworldly figure. He was a neighbor and a friend—who had merely been burning down barns for some undefined motive. The community rallied to his defense, not because it felt Vernon had been wrongfully accused, but instead out of sympathy.

After all, ol' Vern had been well celebrated for his big heart and his penchant for helping folks. He snowplowed neighbors' drives, mowed people's fields, and put out fires as a volunteer, including some of the very ones he had set. He had pulled tree limbs from Heidi Motzkin's yard and freed her snowbound car. Always refusing payment, he joked that he was a "fairy godfather."

"He's the salt of the earth," declared Rose Ann Vincor, whose barn Shultis was caught torching and whose family had had four other barns singed but not successfully burned during the arson spree.

Shultis's supporters, including former victims, rallied around him. They packed the court to demand his bail be reduced to permit him to remain free pending trial. They argued through a letter-writing campaign to lawyers and newspapers that Vernon was a good but troubled man who did not deserve to go to prison. He needed psychiatric help instead.

"It's a very intelligent community," said Town Supervisor Kellogg. "People are looking at this and saying a person needs help and the family needs support. Everybody is saying what he did was wrong. It's another question what the punishment is."

The only person in town who appeared troubled about the turning of the Devil into almost a cult hero was District Attorney Michael Kavanagh.

"I think it's somewhat ironic," he said, "that the

man who was causing so much destruction to the town and was the object of so much fear* is now embraced by some of the community leaders. I think these folks are guilty of leading with their hearts and not with their heads."

---

*Vernon Shultis, electronically monitored and unable to leave his house without permission, is presently undergoing psychiatric testing for pyromania. Indicted for the Woodstock arsons but not convicted, he must be considered innocent until and if he is found guilty.

Chapter

25

Miami Beach, Florida

Pyromaniacs are the most perplexing of fire starters, difficult to understand. While in his fire starter mode, the pyro is not a rational being. He is driven by delusions centering around flame as a sexual or adrenaline stimulant. Psychiatrists have categorized them into various pigeonholes: psychopaths; epileptic amnesiacs who sometimes become irritable, then troublesome, and then start fires; psychoneurotics under emotional tension; the mentally handicapped; alcoholics or drug addicts; fetishists who replace an urge for female clothing, for example, with fire; exhibitionists; Peeping Toms; "heroes" who "discover" and help put out the fire; suppressed homosexuals . . .

The destructive quality of unleashed flames somehow becomes for such people a substitute for something they lack emotionally.

Miami Beach fire investigator Vance Irik has discovered during his 2-decade-long career that if he arrives early at a suspicious fire, he might walk through the crowd of onlookers and pick out the culprit. The pyro is always more intense than other spectators, his eyes bright with excitement. He might go either of two extremes—failing to notice anyone around him or babbling excitedly to whoever will listen. Irik looks for guys with their hands in their pockets, masturbating.

One evening, he rolled on a 9 P.M. pushout to a fleabag hotel on Collins Avenue. It wasn't much of a fire—just a bed fire on the second floor. The bed was a pile of charred mattress and the wall above it was peeled and blackened. Flames had not spread beyond the one room. Residents claimed their lives might have been saved by some guy wearing not a stitch of clothing who scurried from room to room spreading the alarm.

A single pumper remained at the scene for overhaul when Irik arrived. Police had cleared the area so people could go about their normal business. Busy Collins Avenue was opened again to a steady stream of tourist traffic. Spotting movement on the pumper parked in front of a closed clothing store, Irik strolled over to investigate, expecting to find one of the firefighters.

Instead, he froze in his tracks. He blinked and looked around. Instead of a firefighter, a skinny man, stark naked—wearing not even a smile—squatted atop the pumper. He looked old, so much older than any man could be, and haggard, as though he had just constructed the world with his own hands and then destroyed it.

He stared down at Irik. His eyes shone wide, like dark spots of oil. Sand, as from a grave, coated his frail body.

"I'm so terribly sorry," the pale nude began, lips quivering. "I didn't mean to hurt nobody, but I didn't have no choice."

He sounded harmless enough at the moment. Irik looked around for a cop. Seeing none, he edged closer to keep the guy talking and prevent his fleeing. And there the tall uniformed fire cop stood on busy Collins Avenue, holding what appeared to be a normal conversation with a jaybird-naked man standing on the fire engine. People in passing cars gawked as they pointed and laughed.

"I like firefighters," the nude continued in a diminished voice. "I wouldn't want to see any of you get hurt."

What the hell. Irik kept the conversation going. The naked man leaned an elbow on the top handrail. His eyes shifted nervously as, in apparent need to justify himself, he clarified how he had come to be in his present plight.

"The voices told me what to do," he explained, his voice unnaturally calm, considering he could have burned alive 100 or more people. "The voices told me to cleanse myself with fire. But first I had to urinate on myself three times. Then I jerked off and took some cum juice and made a cross on my forehead. That's what the voices told me to do. I knew I had to die too in order to cleanse myself with fire. So I took off the rest of my clothes and lay down on the bed and struck a match to it."

Irik stared, speechless.

"It got so hot in the bed," the nude continued, "that I changed my mind. I couldn't do it."

He jumped up, warned his neighbors, and fled the hotel while his bed blazed. He said the voices ordered him to drown himself instead. He raced to the nearby beach, where he waded into the dark surf and tried to sink. He kept coming up to gasp for breath. Finally, waves washed him onto the sand, where he lay for a while weeping because he was such a failure.

He looked at Irik with his wild, lonely eyes. "I'm glad the hotel didn't burn," he murmured.

"Do you think the goddamned voices lied to me?" he* asked.

---

*The nude man was eventually determined to be criminally insane and institutionalized.

Chapter

26

Miami, Florida

Detective Wil Fuhrman learned that a Miami police patrol officer had spotted a prowler while cruising the warehouse district at about 3 A.M. the morning of the IWDC blaze. He summoned agent Bill Hamilton with an apologetic "I don't know what we've got, if it's anything much. . . ."

"Then it'll fit with everything else we don't have."

The patrolman was a rookie with the looks of a high-school kid. He answered questions in a formal, clipped tone, like he was on the witness stand: "I was on routine patrol on the graveyard shift about an hour before I heard the call come out about the fire. I saw this subject walking on the street a block away from the warehouse. I drove past him."

A guy committing a $12 million crime possibly involving cocaine cartels did not *walk* away from the crime scene. Still, if not a suspect, he could be a witness.

"Did you stop him and get his name?" Hamilton queried. "What did he look like?"

The rookie resumed speaking. "He acted like he knew where he was going. He wasn't drunk or anything.

136

As for description, he was a white guy. I don't think he was Cuban. I know he wasn't black. Not *real* black, anyhow. He was about average in height and weight and his clothing was a mess. He was probably a hab, a vagrant."

"Which way was he going?" Hamilton persisted. "Did he divert his path when he saw you?"

"He was walking north. I don't think he even noticed me. He couldn't have cared less. That's the way habs are. I'd have stopped him for questioning had he acted jumpy or tried to rabbit on me."

"Could you tell if he was injured?"

"Like a burn? That sort of thing? It wasn't like his clothes were smoking. He didn't exactly have a spring to his step, but he didn't walk like he was about to keel over either. Honestly, I didn't pay a whole lot of attention. There are always habs nosing around in there trying to find places to hole up. I didn't see him as suspicious at the time."

Hamilton chided him. "It was *three o'clock* in the morning—"

"If we stopped and checked out every vagrant we saw, that's all we'd be doing all night long. Haven't you looked at the streets lately? The homeless are everywhere; they can beg and sleep where they please, protected by law. After a while, you pay no more attention to them than you do trash thrown on the street. That's just the way it is."

That *is* the way it is. The homeless have to do *something;* otherwise, they blend into the background like old McDonald's wrappers or Budweiser beer cans. Just nasty, filthy vagrants.

One of them managed to wheel his way into the foreground while crossing Biscayne Boulevard in his wheelchair. He was about half drunk and despised the entire world. A northbound 18-wheeler squealed to an unexpected stop and blasted its horn.

That pissed off the hab. He stopped in front of the tractor-trailer.

The trucker honked again.

"Fuck you!" screamed the hab as he faced off against the angry truck driver. He thrust his arm high in the air, middle digit of his hand defiantly extended. It was like the cartoon in which the mouse is giving the eagle the finger as winged death swoops down upon him.

The trucker saw red, along with some colors that may have yet to be discovered. He gunned his big diesel—and smashed the wheelchair and its obnoxious occupant flat.

Chapter

27

Craig, Alaska

Nearly a year after the trawler *Investor* burned almost to her waterline off Egg Island, Lieutenant John Shover and Sergeant Charles Miller attended an inquest in Ketchikan. Thus far, the inability of the coroner to determine the exact number of bodies consumed by the blaze had left detectives with the nagging question of whether one of the crew might have escaped and was therefore the killer.

Coroner Kris Carlisle presided over the inquest jury, before whom forensic pathologists presented findings from their long, trying study of the bones and ashes recovered from *Investor*'s burned hull. They testified that although they could not possibly identify the victims' remains as belonging to particular persons, they were positive now, after due consideration, that *seven* bodies had been removed from the boat. They were all adults. It could be presumed that 4-year-old John Coulthurst, of whom little remained, died along with his father, mother, and sister.

The jury subsequently ruled that all eight persons believed to have been aboard *Investor* were legally dead and that those persons were the four members of the

Coulthurst family and the boat's four crewmen. The ruling cleared the record to show that someone other than those known to have been aboard was the murderer.

Shover and Miller walked outside. It was early spring, but snow remained in patches among the shadows of the firs. Shover thrust his hands deep into his pockets.

"I want this killer," he said. "I want him bad."

Chapter

28

Sapulpa, Oklahoma

News of the charred corpses in the car trunk, along with a description of Michael Houghton's missing Isuzu pickup, flashed across Oklahoma and the nation via radio, newspapers, television, and law-enforcement communications. It struck a responsive public chord, judging from the number of tips police received, all of which had to be diligently checked out.

On Thursday afternoon, October 8, Sapulpa Police Detective Bruce Duncan grabbed his ringing telephone receiver on his way out of the office to follow up on still another lead.

"Yeah? Duncan here."

"Okay. That Isuzu pickup. It's just now leaving Jennings heading for Sapulpa. There's two men in it."

"Who's this? Who are the men driving——?"

The phone buzzed annoyingly—it was disconnected.

Jennings was a small semi–ghost town about 40 miles west of Tulsa. Duncan flashed the alarm to all area law enforcement.

Twenty-seven minutes later, at 5:40 P.M., the Tulsa police dispatcher's office received a second tip. A

141

citizen was listening in on the police band, a favorite pastime in some cities.

"That dead man's pickup . . ." began the caller. "I just saw it headed south on 63rd West Avenue from Charles Page Boulevard in Sand Springs. It looked like there were two men in it."

Sand Springs, another Tulsa suburb, lay west of the city on either side of the Keystone Expressway. Tulsa uniformed patrolmen immediately inundated the Sand Springs line and Charles Page Boulevard. Evening-shift homicide Sergeant Buck Gardner, a broad-shouldered veteran of the crime wars, stalked the boulevard in his plain unmarked Plymouth while his radio crackled with the excitement of cops on the hunt. No Isuzu pickup, no matter its color or vintage, passed through Sand Springs or West Tulsa in the following hour without a hassle.

Tulsa Detective Steve Steele telephoned Duncan, his counterpart in Sapulpa.

"If that was the right pickup," he said, "it seems to have given us the slip here."

"They'd be crazy as hell to roast two people and then drive around in the same county in the dead guy's vehicle," Duncan opined.

Most criminals weren't noted for their superior IQs.

Streetlights started to blink Charles Page into its nighttime ribbon when Buck Gardner stopped at a light and did a double take at a passing blue Isuzu. The little pickup rambled east on Page, crossed the railroad tracks, and headed toward the building rise of downtown Tulsa in the distance. Two men were in it, shadowy forms in the gathering darkness.

Gardner gunned a right and rode up close enough to obtain the truck's tag number—ZPB-626. Christ, the sonsofbitches hadn't even bothered to switch plates. Great arrogance—or great stupidity.

The detective dropped back and tailed the suspects east. Since he had no emergency equipment on the unmarked, he initiated radio coordination to triangulate the Isuzu into a trap.

The Isuzu slowed as it approached the abandoned Capri drive-in theater. *Rocky* was still on the billboard, the theater's last movie. The first *Rocky,* not the sequels. The pickup turned hard right into the darkened lot and doused its lights.

The old drive-in was still fenced. Both the entrance and the exit had steel posts across them to prevent the theater from being turned into a lovers' lane. Radioing his location, Gardner whipped off the boulevard behind the two men, intent on taking the felony bust now. Apparently, they were on to him.

The truck's engine roared suddenly. Its tires squealed. Fishtailing, it shot past the detective.

Gardner spun his wheel and stomped on the gas— and the chase was on—close and dangerous pursuit. They immediately abandoned four-laned Page for the dark and narrow residential streets that intersected it. The vehicles twisting and turning, sliding out at junctions and intersections, the chase proceeded cat-and-dog at speeds up to 80 mph. South on 81st, back east on West 17th.

Most police car chases are brief. This one was no exception. In the dusk of that Thursday evening, the less-experienced driver ahead lost control and spun the truck into a smoking stall.

Any cop who has chased fleeing felons by car knows how fast they can vacate a cornered vehicle. The Isuzu's doors banged open even before it came to a stop. Two men exploded from it.

They were gone, leaping fences and charging across backyards, before the detective could slide into home plate and get out after them.

Sirens from across the western part of the city converged on the site. Police helicopters buzzed around overhead, their miniature suns blazing as full darkness fell. K-9 officers worked their dogs on long leashes, attempting to pick up a spoor. Police radios chattered a description of the two suspects from the brief glimpses Gardner obtained: "Two white males. Suspect number one is seventeen to twenty years old, five-ten or -eleven, weighing between one hundred forty and one hundred fifty pounds. Long brown hair, a scraggly beard. Dressed in a yellow tank top. Suspect number two, about the same age and build. He has long blondish hair, is clean-shaven and may be wearing a dark tank top or sleeveless shirt. Suspects were driving murder victim's vehicle. Considered armed and dangerous."

Three hours later, with full darkness blanketing the city, police gave up the manhunt in defeat. The suspects had somehow managed to escape.

Chapter

29

New York, New York

When Special Fire Marshal Louis Garcia thought of suspects escaping, he thought of Superman, with a little chuckle. Like many cops thrown into the human cesspool of what passed for urban civilization, he was a man of wit and dark humor. His Manhattan beat was like a David Lynch movie—urban chic with dinner parlors and roses on the surface while the underbelly rotted away. Like the beautiful woman having sex with her boyfriend's Doberman.

Summoned to a domestic arson fire in a Manhattan apartment building, the big man laboriously climbed the cruddy stairs to the sixth floor. He passed along the hallway to the scorched apartment at the end. A door cracked open. The wizened face of a diminutive old woman poked out through the crack.

"Psst!" she hissed, eyes darting about looking for signs of danger.

"What?"

"Psst! C'mere."

He walked over.

"Who are you?" she demanded, even though he was in uniform.

"Fire Marshal Garcia. I'm investigating the fire here this morning."

"Watch out for Superman," she whispered.

"Excuse me?"

"Watch out for Superman."

She darted back inside, like a mouse into its hole, and Garcia dismissed her as being one of the city's uncountable kooks.

Someone had sloshed gasoline underneath the door of apartment 603 and ignited it early that morning while the woman inside was still sleeping. Fortunately, other residents stomped it out before the hallway suffered much more than smoke damage.

The apartment's occupant, a woman of about 35, slumped on the sofa looking mildly depressed. She sighed and let tears flow freely as she explained to Garcia about her estranged husband. As recently as 2 weeks earlier, he had piled trash at her door and tossed a match onto it.

"Why wasn't he arrested then?" Garcia asked.

The woman managed a sardonic smile. "Some people call my husband Superman," she said.

Why? Because when police came to arrest him, blocking the exits, he sprinted to the window, threw it open, and looked straight down six stories to the street. He made a motion as if he were flinging aside a cape and announced, in dramatic parody of General Douglas MacArthur, "I shall return."

Then he leaped out the window.

His wife screamed, *"No!"*

She darted to the window, expecting to see her poor goofy husband's bloody body splattered on the concrete below. She stared open-mouthed. Police officers rushed in and stared with her, for instead of dying in the fall, the guy was running away down the street—limping a little, but otherwise apparently uninjured.

Normal people committed suicide by jumping from sixth-floor windows.

After that, the old lady down the hall assumed the duty of warning policemen about him.

"Psst! Watch out for Superman.* He'll fly out the window and get away."

---

*"Superman" was eventually arrested and served a short jail sentence.

Chapter

30

After Bill Clinton was elected to the presidency, he ordered a truce on the War on Drugs waged by the previous two presidents, trimmed $9 million from the Coast Guard's drug interdiction budget, disbanded the federal drug task force, and essentially called a halt to special operations against drug traffickers. He announced the United States' emphasis on fighting the drug problem would from now on stress "education and rehabilitation."

"The War on Drugs is now officially over," declared a Coast Guard commander. "We haven't won. We surrendered to the smugglers. Give things a year and smugglers will be transporting shiploads of cocaine into the country stacked on their weather decks, just like they did before we declared war on them."

The nation immediately experienced the effects of the war's end. In Florida, the center of the smuggling trade, tractor-trailer trucks brought in acetone and other chemicals to process cocaine for market while other tractor-trailers hauled away the finished product to disappear up the noses of cokeheads all over the United States. Greater availability drove up drug

Arson may be started for revenge, for profit, for excitement, for recognition, out of fear, and to cover up other crimes. *(Bureau of Alcohol, Tobacco and Firearms)*

In spite of today's high-tech crime investigations, the shovel is still the fire cop's most indispensable tool. Here, ATF arson investigators work to solve a whodunit in Miami. *(Bureau of Alcohol, Tobacco and Firearms)*

Miami fire-for-insurance blaze at the International Warehouse Distributing Corporation pitted the wits of veteran fire cops Rocky McAllister, Bill Hamilton, and Wil Fuhrman against professional arsonists in a case that led them from Canada to South America. *(Metro-Dade Fire Department)*

Detective Wil Fuhrman, Metro-Dade Police Department arson investigator. *(Courtesy of Wil Fuhrman)*

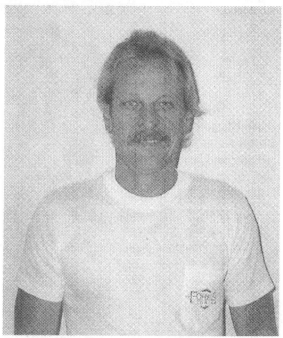

BATF arson investigator Bill Hamilton. *(Courtesy of William Hamilton)*

Captain Bill "Rocky" McAllister, head of the Metro-Dade Fire Department's arson squad. *(Courtesy of W.A. McAllister)*

Thomas Jefferson Midkiff, convicted of the brutal slaughter of Sheila Ring and her two-year-old daughter, Jasmine Sutphin, in a love affair gone sour, ending literally in flames. *(Carroll County Sheriff's Department)*

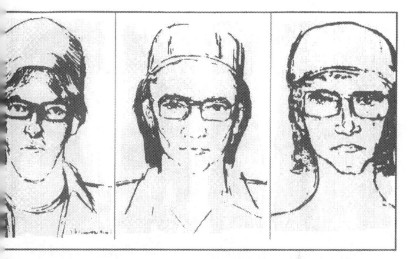

Mark and Irene Coulthurst, along with their two small children and four crew members, were immolated by fire at sea aboard their commercial fishing boat, *Investor*. Alaska State Police released this multiple-witness composite of suspect seen fleeing the burning vessel. *(Alaska State Police)*

Bodies shown stacked up outside the Happy Land Social Club arson, which killed 87 nightclubbers. It was the biggest mass murder in U.S. history prior to the Oklahoma City bombing. *(New York City Police)*

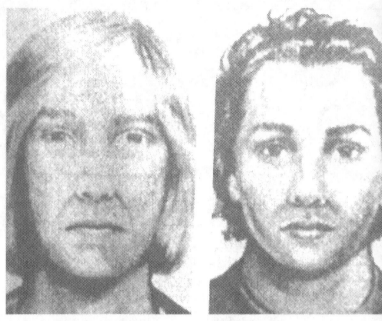

Tulsa, Oklahoma, police released this composite of Scott Allen Hain (left) and Robert Wayne Lambert, who were convicted for kidnapping Laura Lee Sanders and William Houghton and burning them alive in the trunk of their car. *(Tulsa Police Department)*

Tulsa, Oklahoma, Detective Steve Steele worked with fire marshals to end crime spree of Scott Allen Hain and Robert Wayne Lambert. *(Author photo)*

Branch Davidian complex burning near Waco, Texas, killing 81 people, including 25 children. One of the most notorious cases of self-immolating arson in U.S. history. *(Bureau of Alcohol, Tobacco and Firearms)*

David Koresh, leader of the religious cult Branch Davidian. *(Bureau of Alcohol, Tobacco and Firearms)*

Fire Investigator Ike Anderson sifts through ashes of house fire near Live Oak, Florida, that took the lives of elderly blind woman Mabel Thompson, her two blind sons, and her blind daughter. Evidence led to the arrest of her ex-convict son-in-law. *(Florida Bureau of Fire and Arson Investigation)*

Curtis Foster Jr. being led to trial in Muskogee, Oklahoma, on charges that he torched his residence, murdering his wife, two daughters, and two stepchildren. *(Photo courtesy of Muskogee Daily Phoenix)*

abuse; use of drugs, especially cocaine, nearly doubled among teenagers. It is sometimes estimated that the value of all cocaine and marijuana bootlegged into the United States would pay off the entire national debt within 2 years.

A surprising offshoot of increased drug abuse is an unmistakable correlation between arson and drugs, as there is a similar correlation between drugs and other crimes. Those states with the highest drug abuse rates also have the highest arson rates. California, not surprisingly, ranks first in arson, followed by New York, Texas, Michigan, and Pennsylvania. Florida ranks sixth. David Lowery, chief fire investigator in Charlotte, North Carolina, attributed the 1% increase in arson nationwide and the 8% increase in the Northeast alone to arson's relationship with the greater availability of drugs.

Most drug-related arsons are petty hit-and-miss crimes, such as the doper who set fire to a handicapped woman after he lost $50 in a rock cocaine deal, or the four men who crashed their car into the lobby of an apartment house and set it afire in retaliation against residents who complained of their drug dealing. All fire cops, however, experience the drug–arson alliance in some form.

In Miami, old fire horse Rocky McAllister found it difficult to resist the clanging of the alarm. Already in the field, he overheard the radio dispatcher assign a pushout to a residential fire nearby. He rolled on it.

The involved house was a quarter-million-dollar monstrosity. Smoke fouled the entire neighborhood, churning from the house and twisting like a tornado. Although firefighters attacked valiantly, it was obvious to McAllister that the house was a goner.

A guy roared up the street in a blue Mercedes, jumped out hysterically, and charged toward the house. A truckie ran over to help McAllister restrain the nut.

"What the hell are you *doing?*" McAllister bawled. Flames whipped at them. "You crazy or what?"

"This is my house——"

"There's nothing you can do in there except kill yourself."

The firefighters had to physically drag him back.

"You don't understand," he protested. "I *have* to get in the house."

He hesitated, then suddenly blurted out, "My house-keeper was supposed to be here."

That put a different focus on things. Time was essential, as the fire was rapidly engulfing the structure. McAllister organized a rescue patrol armed with a 2 ½-inch pipe. A frontal assault and interior penetration always proved difficult and hazardous because of its inherent threat of backdrafts and flashovers.

"The roof could fall in at any moment," the fire commander warned. "Get in there——*then get out!*"

McAllister imagined he heard the dry, hollow laughter of Fate as, hose charged, he and his crew advanced behind their stream of water. Flames bent and lapped out windows and around eaves and tongued through the roof. Tremendous heat blasting from the open door and a busted picture window boiled like the open maw of a giant furnace. The hallway inside along which the fighters advanced was a bed of coals hissing like a nest of vipers. A wall collapsed with a resounding crash. The ceiling panted for breath. Smoke reduced visibility to an arm's length——sometimes not even that.

After searching the living room, kitchen, dining room, and bathroom and coming up empty-handed, the rescuers fought their way from bedroom to bedroom. The last door along the hallway was locked. The ax man chopped through it. A firestorm raged inside around a stack of boxes. Clouds of fine crystal spewed from the boxes into the supercharged air, igniting into glorious bursts of sparkling blues and greens shot through with purples and reds. McAllister felt like he had stepped into the aurora borealis.

His awe turned to anger. "Let this shit burn!" he bellowed, jabbing his gloved thumb toward the exit. "Out. *Out.*"

The roof heaved, sighed, and crackled. Sections of it collapsed behind the retreating firemen.

Captain McAllister was known by all his colleagues as a man with a ready smile and a kind word. He had neither, however, as he burst out of the fire two steps ahead of death. He shucked his SCBA. His thick hands knotted into fists as he lunged at the home owner.

"There's no one in that house and you *knew* it!" he raged. "You dirty son of a bitch. You sent us in there to risk getting killed because you thought we might save your damned *cocaine.*"

In New York, Fire Marshal Louis Garcia's run-in with arson and drugs took on a certain sad and melancholy character. In investigating a suspicious three-alarm fire on the thirteenth floor of a ramshackle SRO Hotel in the Bronx, he learned of a business arrangement between two welfare mamas and three young black street studs called Born, Flip, and Science. The street studs supplied crack cocaine to the welfare mamas, who sold it on the streets.

Born sauntered into the hotel the day before the fire to collect money from his crack bitches. When they refused to cough up any dough, the infuriated Born snatched one of the women's little daughters and pressed a gun muzzle against the child's temple. He threatened to shoot her unless he got his money.

Born seethed all night, even though the women paid up. The next day, he brought Science and Flip with him to the hotel to beat up the bitches and teach them a lesson. They also intended to strong-arm $300 owed them by other crackheads on the thirteenth floor. One of the dopers was spaced enough to tell Science to fuck off. That did it. Science lit up an apartment in retaliation as residents fled in terror.

When the case finally came to trial, the little girl Born threatened to shoot walked over to Garcia. She was a timid, brown little creature of about 7 with entwined fingers and big soulful eyes.

"Officer Garcia," she begged, "please take me home with you."

Frustrated as fire cops become over drug arsons, fire investigator Ron Shinnen of the Tulsa, Oklahoma, fire department found himself placed in the unusual position of sympathizing with a fire starter who burned down a vacant house in his north-side neighborhood. As firefighters fought to extinguish the 2:15 A.M. blaze in the single-story house, out of which tenants had moved the day before, Shinnen questioned neighbors to determine if they had seen anything unusual. The odor of gasoline permeated the burning house.

William Ramon Risby, 49, lived a few houses down the block. Shinnen noticed an empty gasoline can on the porch. Risby also stank of gasoline fumes. Pressed, he soon confessed that he had indeed set the blaze.

Why?

"The crackheads," he explained. "Looky here—there's several vacant houses around and they're all filled with bums and dope dealers. The police can't do nothing. As soon as a house goes vacant, the dope dealers move in and crackheads start stealing everything you ain't got nailed down. I don't want them dope dealers on my block—so I burned down the house before they could move in."

It was hard to argue with logic like that.

"I feel compassion for him," Shinnen confided to

police officers as they hauled Risby* off to jail. "I can understand his wanting to remove a problem in his neighborhood. He knows he screwed up and that what he did was wrong, but he said he had to get rid of the drugs."

One of the cops groused, "Maybe he should have waited until after the dealers moved in before he burned the house."

---

*Born, Flip, and Science were convicted of first-degree arson and served short prison sentences. William Ramon Risby was convicted of second-degree arson and sentenced to 5 years in prison.

Chapter

31

Unknown to the fire cops stalled in their investigation of the IWDC fire, the federal Drug Enforcement Administration (DEA) also had an interest in acetone. Narcs were immediately suspicious of anyone purchasing hundreds of gallons of the stuff. It generally meant someone was in business manufacturing narcotics. If the agents were diligent and everything went according to script, the acetone, the players, and a big load of cocaine all intersected at some secret drug lab.

DEA agents Jeff Harrison and his partner A. B. Duquette drew the acetone assignment and the stakeout on the residence of the guy who bought the big supply. It was up to them to discover where the acetone was presently stored and what it was being used for. The best way to do that without blowing their cover and causing the suspects to scatter like rabbits was to keep the bad guys under surveillance.

The two agents began their surveillance on August 31, three days *before* the IWDC warehouse burned. There was nothing dark or sinister about the target. The house was a modest little bungalow in a northwest Miami neighborhood where residents often parked

154

their vehicles alongside the curbless street and left bicycles on front lawns. Smugglers higher in the doper hierarchy seemed to be average Joes on average blocks with average lives. Few were obvious scumbuckets like the street pushers.

Harrison once busted a major player in a mob-run drug ring who lived in a fine neighborhood near Greynolds Park. The elderly, white-haired gentleman was a well-liked and respected fixture in his community. His arrest came as a big shock to his neighbors, sort of like discovering a serial killer living next door.

"He's such a quiet, decent man," they said. "The kids on the block go over and swim in his pool."

Harrison had seen too many like him over the years. It jaded him. He sometimes teased his younger partner Duquette about his idealism. What a crock to think they really made a shitpot full of difference in the international drug trade. Drug law enforcement in Florida was like being a gravedigger during the Dark Ages and the Black Plague: there was always more work than you could ever do, corpses continued to stack up, and the job stunk.

He sat behind the wheel of the parked nondescript 6-year-old Chevy down the street from the target. The undercover's windows were darkly tinted to conceal the two men inside from all but the most observant passerby; it blended in with the other cars parked on the street. Harrison, who was nearing retirement, was shorter and thinner than Duquette. He had affected a scraggly ponytail to help him blend in undercover and developed a bit of a paunch from too many days and nights parked on stakeout like this waiting for some scumbag to make a move, when all a guy could do was sit and consume munchies to stay awake—or, as in Duquette's case, smoke cigarettes one after the other.

Duquette used to play football for Boston University and worked a couple of years as a street cop with the Miami–Dade Police Department before hiring on with

DEA. He honestly thought he was fighting for Law and Order, Justice, and the American Way.

Harrison stretched and reached for a bag of Fritos as the sun dropped low toward the Everglades. He cracked his side windows to let his big partner's cigarette smoke escape.

"Why can't you munch doughnuts like other cops?" he complained.

"I would if they made them with nicotine icing. It's the job. I didn't start smoking until I came on DEA."

The two men settled into a companionable silence. You could only talk so much football or police work or babes before you ran out of things to say. Duquette grumbled, "My ass is nibbling a hole through the seat."

An hour or so later, after nightfall, a white Ford step van entered the opposite end of the street and eased down the block behind the wide illumination of its headlamps. The agents slid low in their seat. The van stopped in front of the targeted bungalow. One man got out and opened the garage door. The driver backed the van inside. The garage door closed. Duquette sighed.

"Now we wait some more," Harrison said with a wry grin.

"More waiting? How novel. Let's try that."

A short while later, the van nosed back out of the garage and returned in the direction from which it arrived. Harrison maneuvered the Chevy onto the next block and picked up the van's taillights three blocks farther over to avert suspicion.

"At least we're not house-sitting for them on our dead asses," he said.

Most dopers are paranoid. Afraid of being followed, they cut all kinds of switchbacks and tricks to lose a possible tail. One dealer in north Dade doubled back and shot a salesman in the face because the poor slob just happened to be going the same direction as he. The van, however, was easy. Boring.

It picked up the Palmetto Expressway south and

exited onto the Airport Expressway. It exited again almost immediately into a darkened warehouse area at the west end of Miami International Airport. Big-time dealers often rented warehouses for their operations.

"Maybe it's leading us to the mother lode for the narcotics trade in Dade County," Duquette quipped.

"Can't be. City Hall is in the other direction."

The van drove straight to a Ryder truck rental at the edge of the warehouse district. Harrison backed the Chevy into a nearby alley and the agents waited. Presently, the van drove away from the Ryder, followed by a 2-ton rental.

The two vehicles beelined to the bungalow in northwest Miami. The van nosed into the garage and the Ryder backed into the driveway. The drivers entered the house.

"I'm about out of cigarettes," Duquette complained. "Do you think we can get delivery service?"

The next afternoon when Duquette and Harrison took over from their day-shift relief, Duquette fished out four packs of cigarettes and stacked them on the dash within easy reach, in preparation for a long night. Neither the van nor the Ryder had budged all day.

Action began right away. One of the men came out of the house and left in the Ryder. The narcs tagged it to a warehouse in south Miami. They watched at a distance through binoculars while it picked up a load of empty 5-gallon hard-plastic chemical-safe jugs, then returned to the bungalow and parked as before.

"The acetone may already be in the garage," Harrison surmised.

"Could be this *is* the lab," Duquette suggested. "What better cover story than a sleepy little street and a mom-and-pop-and–apple pie neighborhood? Acetone comes in fifty-five-gallon drums. Maybe they're gonna use the five-gallon jugs to transport acetone to *here* from somewhere else."

"Makes sense."

Duquette decided to cop a peek inside the closed garage after nightfall by pretending to be a neighbor out for a stroll. He sauntered down one side of the street, then returned via the bungalow and the parked Ryder.

Harrison watched his partner pause in front of the house and pull a deep speculative drag from his cigarette. After a burglarlike glance all around, he flipped the cigarette into the street and darted into the shadows alongside the garage.

Every dog in the neighborhood seemed to start barking all at once in chorus. Duquette reappeared immediately. He forced himself to look casual. He walked past the Chevy and on around the corner, to deceive anyone who might be watching. He sneaked back to the car minutes later.

"Damned big Doberman," he fussed. "I thought the sumbitch was coming over the fence to take a bite outta my ass. There aren't any windows in the garage. I couldn't see shit."

On the third day of surveillance, September 2, DEA agents decided to concentrate on the bungalow instead of tailing the Ryder and the van all over the city. They were convinced a drug lab was being constructed inside the garage. Harrison and Duquette's day relief logged that one man left in the Ryder, presumably to bring back acetone after unloading some of the 5-gallon containers inside the garage and keeping some inside the truck. The Ryder did not return.

The van came and left several times, the last time after dark. Harrison watched it leave. He nudged Duquette.

"Something is about to go down," he said. "I think we ought to hit 'em with a search warrant soon, instead of just sitting here night after night."

Duquette lit up a cigarette. Harrison cracked his window.

"I'll give them up when I retire," Duquette said, "and only drink a glass of wine a day and play golf."

"You won't make it to retirement at the rate you're going."

"My grandma smoked until she died at the age of ninety-one." He paused to chuckle. "She was walking back from the IGA with a half gallon of milk, a big can of peaches, and a carton of Winstons when she was run over by a Cadillac."

"Tell me you're kidding."

"In a way, you could say smoking finally killed her. She was fishing in the bag for a smoke and didn't see the Cadillac until it was too late."

That same night, at approximately 4 A.M., American Airlines passengers witnessed an explosion they first took to be an airplane crashing among warehouses west of the airport. DEA made no connection between the explosion there and the acetone stash they thought they had under surveillance in south Miami.

Chapter

32

Recovering, coordinating, and accurately interpreting evidence in crimes of arson and finally pinning the crime to a suspect is never a sure procedure. That is why only about 15% of all arsons successfully result in prosecution. Many suspicious fires remain simply that—*suspicious*. Others take years to solve, are never solved, or are attributed to an innocent party.

One such innocent party could be Catherine O'Leary, whose case may finally be cleared after more than 125 years. She was at home in bed as she claimed, rather than milking her infamous cow in the barn, when the legendary great Chicago fire of October 8, 1871, started and leveled more than 3 square miles of the city. At least that is what lawyer–amateur historian–sleuth Dick Bales put forth in an investigation he presented to the Illinois State Historical Society.

An official panel conducted an inquiry after the fire, finally blaming Mrs. O'Leary and her cow for accidentally starting the fire when the cow knocked over her lantern. Mrs. O'Leary denied it vehemently. She claimed until she died that she was home in bed when the fire started.

Bales studied more than 1,000 pages of the hearing transcript before concluding that the inquiry was sloppily conducted and that the panel overlooked or dismissed contradictory evidence and did little follow-up. He then obtained tract records of the city before the fire from Chicago Title Insurance Company. Historians have long wanted to draw an exact map of O'Leary's neighborhood, but until Bales came up with the tract records, they had nothing to go on but a few old photographs and a newspaper report. Public records had burned in the blaze.

If not Mrs. O'Leary, then *who* was responsible for igniting the fire that almost destroyed the city?

Bales points the finger of suspicion at an O'Leary neighbor named Daniel "Peg Leg" Sullivan.

"I started thinking that there are holes in Peg Leg's testimony," Bales said, "and they should be pretty easy to check out."

Sullivan told the investigating panel that he was sitting in front of another neighbor's house when he saw the glow of fire in O'Leary's barn. He said he ran to the barn, where he struggled to free livestock trapped inside the structure. He managed to free one calf before he ran to get help.

Using the long-unknown tract records, Bales drew the entire O'Leary block to scale. The re-created De-Koven Street on the west side supports his conclusion.

To begin with, a two-story house stood between the barn and the neighbor's house in front of which Sullivan claimed he was sitting. He could not have seen the fire from his location until the blaze all but consumed the barn.

He was 200 feet away from the barn. Fire experts determined that fire rapidly enveloped the barn, that it was totally involved within mere minutes. Peg Leg's nickname derived from an obvious physical impairment—he only had one leg while its opposite was a whittled stick of oak. There was no way, Bales argued, even granting that Sullivan saw the fire as he claimed, that an impaired man had enough time to hobble across an unevenly paved street "into a burning barn full of hay and wood shavings, struggle to free the animals, fall down but still ultimately free a calf *without being injured,"* as he had testified. That was a lot of running in a short time for an old man with a wooden leg.

Sullivan, Bales said, lied to the investigating panel.

Bales theorizes Sullivan, not Mrs. O'Leary, was in the barn that night to feed his own family's cow, and that it was he, not Mrs. O'Leary, who dropped a match, pipe, or lantern to ignite the legendary blaze that swept across Chicago. In the meantime, the much-maligned Mrs. O'Leary was home in bed asleep, as she claimed.

An additional theory suggests the fire might have been arson—that Peg Leg Sullivan deliberately set the fire for motives unknown.

"It is a very careful and responsible job of research, which hasn't always been true of speculation about how the fire started," said Northwestern University Professor Carl Smith of Bales's research. "But it's like all other ideas about the fire. It's still simply a theory that cannot be proven by a confession or credible eyewitness accounts."

Chapter

33

Craig, Alaska

The *Investor* burned on September 6. A year later, during the following fishing season, a young man named Tom Bias telephoned state trooper headquarters in Ketchikan. The case by that time had fallen into follow-up investigation by Sergeant James Stogsdill, although Lieutenant John Shover and Sergeant Charles Miller retained a vested interest in it. The detectives sometimes got together over coffee to discuss the case, but months had passed without a single new lead. It appeared all chances of catching the mass killer had gone up in smoke with the fishing boat.

Stogsdill held the telephone receiver on his shoulder with his chin while he rapidly scribbled notes on a pad. The conversation would require a face-on follow-up, but for now Stogsdill's broad features gradually lost their scowl of skepticism as Tom Bias talked.

"I'm back in Alaska for the fishing season," he explained, "and I happened to see that poster showing a sketch of who you think burned the fishing boat *Investor*. I'm almost certain I recognize the guy."

Yeah. Right. How many calls had detectives received that started out exactly like that?

Bias further explained that he and the suspect were crewing on the fishing boat *Blue Fin* that year of the murders when she put in for the weekend at Craig for fuel and supplies.

"There was a hell of a lot of excitement in town that night," he said. Several fishing boats were in port, their crews letting loose a little in the bars and restaurants. "We put out early the next morning and heard by radio only that there had been some people aboard the *Investor* and that they had burned to death."

Blue Fin followed the running fish across the Gulf of Alaska to Kodiak and then on to Bristol Bay. The suspect left the boat on Kodiak and caught a bush flight to the mainland. He said he had called Bellingham, Washington, and learned there was some sort of family crisis that required his going home fast. Another crew member had to be hired to take his place.

"I don't know much about the guy," Bias concluded. "I only first met him when he signed aboard for the season. I'm afraid I don't even remember his name."

That was easy enough to find out. Fishing vessels were required to register with the state. After hanging up with Bias, Stogsdill made several phone calls to run down the owner and captain of the *Blue Fin,* who was again fishing Alaskan waters. Ship-to-shore radio communications finally linked the detective with the salty captain.

"I think you're smelling the wrong fish if you think that young fella could have killed those people aboard *Investor,*" he growled. "He seemed to be a real nice kid, and I doubt if he would have left us if there hadn't been trouble at home. In fact, I think he fished with Mark Coulthurst a couple of seasons."

"You're probably right," the detective conceded. "What's his name?"

Raymond Joe Litzch. The name had not surfaced before.

"It looks like it might be coming together," Stogsdill reported to Lieutenant Shover.

"Don't set your hopes too high," Shover cautioned. They had been to this point several times before.

A homicide investigation is a remarkable thing in that it may continue for days, weeks, even years with every clue, every lead drifting into oblivion. But, then, when the proper piece comes along and everything starts to come together, it comes together rapidly. Detectives are always amazed *afterward* at how well all the pieces fit.

The working out of the tip about Litzch commenced with a rush. Stogsdill sent troopers to Bellingham to uncover everything they could about Litzch, by then 24 years old. Stogsdill's and Shover's hopes rose correspondingly with each new revelation phoned back to headquarters.

Litzch *was* acquainted with Mark Coulthurst; he had fished two previous seasons with Coulthurst before the captain purchased the *Investor*. He appeared in a photograph of Coulthurst and his fishing crew. He even showed up at a memorial service for Mark and his family in Bellingham after they were murdered.

"Ray had nothing to do with this," a Litzch relative adamantly insisted. "When he learned the Coulthursts were burned aboard their boat, he said how sorry he was and that he hoped whoever had done such a thing would burn in hell forever. And if he did it, what kind of a person must he be? It makes me sick to think of it."

The footwork continued. Witnesses who had seen the suspect in the skiff—two from the cannery, one at the time the skiff was abandoned at Craig—identified Raymond Joe Litzch. So did the witness who sold him two jugs of gasoline. Alaskan detectives obtained warrants for the Washington man, charging him with arson and eight counts of first-degree murder. A pair of Bellingham detectives served the warrants, taking into

165

custody the slim young man at a construction job where he worked as a laborer.

"I wouldn't do something like this!" he protested. "What do you think I am? Mark was my friend."

One of Litzch's buddies on the job nodded thoughtfully when questioned. "I thought it was strange that he was working here instead of going fishing where he could have earned a lot more money," he said. "He told me he was through with fishing and never wanted to see Alaska again."

Litzch refused to talk about the crime, except to proclaim his innocence. Lieutenant Shover heaved a long sigh of relief. "If he hadn't been seen and we weren't able to obtain a sketch of him from the descriptions given by the witnesses," he said, "it might have been the perfect crime and never been solved."

In actuality, however, the crime was far from perfect. If police speculation was correct, what turned out to be eight horrendous murders and the torching of a new fishing boat began as a simple theft that turned into one bungle after another.

Shover's theory held that since Litzch had once crewed for Coulthurst, it was natural for him to visit the boat when his own vessel put ashore. The *Investor* was the talk of the town. No one seemed aboard the boat on Sunday evening when Litzch arrived. The Coulthurst family and two of the crew were at the restaurant celebrating Mark's birthday. The other two crewmen might have been sleeping below.

According to Shover's theory, Litzch entered the main cabin topside. Tempted, he began gathering valuables to steal, including Mark's .223 rifle. The crewmen from belowdecks might have heard the noise. Coming topside to investigate, they surprised the thief and confronted him. He shot them with the rifle to avoid apprehension.

That started the ripple effect.

He dragged the two dead men to their quarters and

placed them in their bunks, hoping their deaths would be overlooked until after the *Blue Fin*, and Litzch with it, put to sea the next morning. Only in a mixture of ill timing and fate, the Coulthursts and the other two crewmen returned from celebrating. Hiding below, by now undoubtedly desperate and already twice a murderer, he shot the third and fourth fishermen as they entered below quarters in the darkness.

That still left Mark and Irene Coulthurst and their children between him and escape. The ripple had turned into a tidal wave. Bursting out from belowdecks, he mowed down the captain and his wife, then finished off the children. No witness must be left alive to finger him. Instead of a mere thief, Raymond Joe Litzch became Alaska's worst mass murderer of the century.

Perhaps, aboard a boat in the darkness with eight fresh corpses, he felt momentarily stunned by the enormity of what he had done. Then, like a wild animal trapped, he began looking for a way out.

He had to know he would become an immediate suspect if he was seen leaving the boat or dock that night and the bodies were discovered in the morning. He decided to take the *Investor* out and sink her to bury the evidence of his crime in the cold, dark Alaskan waters, then escape in the skiff, but it would create suspicion if he tried to leave that night.

It must have been a long, sleepless night for him aboard in the dark with the ghosts of the people he had so recently murdered.

At first light, he lowered the tielines that warped *Investor* to *Decade* and put out into the bay with his macabre cargo. He anchored her at Egg Island, 1 mile away. It appeared logical that he might have taken the craft to some distant point to scuttle her—except he realized he had to return to Craig and take sail with his own boat to avoid being tarred with suspicion.

Mark Coulthurst had been so safety-conscious that he filled the hull of his boat with flotation material.

Unable to sink her, Litzch apparently decided to burn her instead. Since there was no ready accelerant aboard, he used the skiff to motor back into town to buy gasoline. This was the mistake that resulted in his being seen by the cannery workers and the attendant at the marina where he purchased gasoline. He was seen again after he set *Investor* afire and beached the skiff at Craig.

His mistakes followed him for nearly 2 years—until they cornered him.* He *would* see Alaska again, but not from the deck of a fishing boat. However, if the crime could be considered far from perfect, so was the case against the only viable suspect to have surfaced during the nearly 2 years of the investigation. Shover himself, though convinced investigators had the right man, admitted the evidence was largely circumstantial.

---

*Charged with the murders of eight victims, Litzch was twice acquitted of charges. Raymond Joe Litzch is not the actual name of the suspect in this crime. In addition, *Blue Fin* is not the true name of the fishing vessel he served aboard. Both have been changed to disguise and protect the suspect's identity, since no purpose is served in his further public exposure. Under the American system of justice, a person acquitted of a crime must be considered innocent. Officially, the macabre case of the *Investor* and her ill-fated crew remains open and unsolved.

Chapter
34

Sapulpa, Oklahoma

Sapulpa Detective Bruce Duncan drove into Jennings shortly after daybreak. The town was merely a shadow of what it had once been. Small towns all over America were losing populations to the megacities. Many of the Jennings buildings were boarded up. Others looked about to be boarded up. A mangy hound crossed the road and grass grew out of the sidewalks.

The tipster who had telephoned in information about the two men in the Isuzu lived in a bleached white shack one block off the main street. Weeds grew around the house. An old Chevrolet sat on blocks in the yard, its engine missing. A lanky, unshaven man spitting from a dip of Skoal came out and sat on the porch.

"I know what you are," he said when Duncan flashed his shield. "I wouldn't normally be talkin' to you at all. But this ain't stealin' something from Wal-Mart. This is *serious* shit, burnin' somebody alive in a car trunk."

"It's serious shit," Duncan admitted.

The informant appeared to want to say what he had to say and then get rid of the detective. In certain neighborhoods, a guy's reputation was damaged irreparably if it was even rumored he had spoken to a cop.

"Them dudes was acquaintances of mine," he began quickly. "I wouldn't exactly call 'em friends. They come up here drivin' that Isuzu pickup last Tuesday mornin' right after sunup."

That would have been October 6, shortly after police discovered Laura Lee's Oldsmobile Cutlass aflame in the field.

"I seen some restaurant work clothes hangin' in the pickup. They hang around here just a little while and then struck out for Wichita, Kansas. They go up to Wichita all the time. After they done left, I got to puttin' two and two together, know what I mean, Dean? I seen on TV about that boy and girl burned up in the car trunk and about how that ol' boy's pickup was missing. Well, sir, when them boys come back from Wichita and stopped by yesterday, I got to thinkin' some more. So I called the law on 'em."

He spat a stream of brown juice at a hen clucking by. Hit it square in the eye. It squawked and ran off.

"You ought to give up that habit," Duncan said. "One of these days your lip'll fall off and you'll step on it."

Back in Tulsa, Duncan compared notes with Tulsa Detective Steve Steele. With names now attached to the two suspects, it was more or less a routine matter to match latent fingerprints from the recovered stolen Isuzu to Scott Allen Hain and Robert Wayne "Bobby" Lambert. Hain was 17, Lambert 21, and both had long criminal histories. In fact, Hain was at the moment an escapee from a juvenile center, while ex-convict Lambert had recently been granted an early release from the Oklahoma State Penitentiary, owing to overcrowding.

During follow-up background on the two men, detectives learned from the executive director of Tulsa-based Rader Children's Diagnostic and Evaluation Center that Scott Hain had a drug problem and that he had been confined to the "kiddie prison" nearly 2 years before because he repeatedly stole cars and was deemed a delinquent for committing burglaries.

"He never really showed any violent behavior," the executive director said.

Three months earlier, on July 1, Hain bolted from a car driven by a juvenile-center escort. It was his second escape. Four more of his fellow juvenile detainees had also escaped and subsequently been charged with new crimes of rape, shooting with intent to kill, and auto theft.

"The kids today, they're more hard-core, more violent," the executive director said in apology. "They have demonstrated they are a real threat to the community."

"No shit, Dick Tracy," Steele grumbled. "Where'd you get your first clue?"

As for Bobby Lambert, he had been charged numerous times with crimes ranging from armed robbery and burglary to auto theft and public drunkenness. He was also a drug addict. He had been released from prison the previous April on an "early out" owing to the so-called Oklahoma Cap Law, which allowed inmates serving time for "nonviolent" crimes to be freed when state prisons reached 95% capacity. Between 400 and 500 convicts were released monthly when the Cap Law was in effect. A shocking number of them soon returned to prison for new crimes. The same shocking number were then rereleased under the Cap Law.

By coincidence, Steve Steele had returned the previous month from a seminar in Nashville on the serial criminal, where seasoned cops from San Diego to New York had brought with them bloodcurdling tales of amputated heads, ground-up torsos, mutilated bodies, fire sacrifice and devil worship. They distributed descriptions of murderers and rapists who committed atrocities and then moved on.

From July to September, Wichita, Kansas, had been

171

plagued by a team of two men who kidnapped, raped, and committed sodomy against at least five Wichita women. The rapes were so brutal, the Wichita cops said, that it was only a matter of time until someone was killed.

"The community as a whole has been in fear," said Kerry Crisp of the Wichita Police Department. "These were brutal team rapes. A lot of people are scared to go out at night."

Steele studied mug shots of Lambert and Hain. He placed them next to composite sketches distributed by Wichita of that city's serial rapists. As recently as 2 weeks before, on September 24, two loud-mouthed, gun-wielding men forced their way into the Tulsa home of Donna Hale on North Florence Place. They beat Hale's boyfriend with a hammer, rummaged through the house for jewelry and cash, and then fled, taking Donna Hale with them.

That was at 6:45 A.M. Two hours later, a blood-soaked woman stumbled up to a house near Sapulpa. Donna Hale told police a frightening tale of how she had been raped by her assailants, beaten with a claw-hammer, and left for dead alongside the highway.

Her descriptions of the suspects and their MO so closely matched those of the Wichita rapists that there could be little doubt that the crimes, occurring 200 miles apart, were related.

Two weeks after Donna Hale was attacked, Sapulpa Sergeant Harley Hausam spotted Laura Lee's Oldsmobile burning in a field a short distance away from where Donna had been booted out.

"We're looking at the same two dirtbags for all these crimes," Steele concluded, showing the photos and sketches to Duncan. Duncan nodded.

The detectives immediately issued a nationwide request to have the murder suspects apprehended. During the next few days as the sleuths pulled in more information and evidence, Lambert and Hain became strong suspects in at least a dozen separate crimes ranging from murder, rape, and robbery to burglary and escape from a penal institution. Steele and Duncan pounded the nighttime streets, trying to find under which rock the pair hid.

Sergeant Steele briefed his homicide supervisor, Sgt. Wayne Allen.

"The longer we look into it," he said, "the more crimes we connect them with. Their MO is to go through backyards after dark peeking into windows looking for people to rob and rape. They're serial criminals operating in Kansas and Oklahoma. They've murdered two people. If we don't nab them soon, I suspect we're going to be chasing *serial murderers.*"

Chapter

35

Miami, Florida

BATF's Bill Hamilton and Metro–Dade fire cops Rocky McAllister and Wil Fuhrman discovered that tracing sales of acetone in Florida was akin to attempting to find a particular raindrop in a thunderstorm. There was simply too much dope activity in the Miami area. Certainly, a multi*billion*-dollar industry blizzarding the United States with Caribbean snow—cocaine—had access to secret sources of processing and distributing materials like acetone.

Hamilton expended hours of valuable time on the telephone attempting to pinpoint CanChem. All that got him was telephone ear. He started out asking his computer for chemical retailers and container manufacturers in the city. He soon expanded the parameters to include the state, then the nation and, finally, the English-speaking globe. He was on the verge of giving up after weeks of hacking when, unexpectedly, it appeared on the screen.

CanChem.

Glowing like a neon light. Canadian Chemicals. Why hadn't he thought of that? The printout provided a

174

Toronto address and telephone number. Hamilton dialed with bated anticipation.

The phone rang on the other end, but no one answered. A glance at his watch informed him the time was only 7 A.M.; he had already been working an hour. Since criminals punched no time clocks, cops couldn't punch them either.

He called Rocky McAllister's number. Another conscientious early riser, Rocky was out on a call to an apartment house fire in Coconut Grove. Hamilton, restless, drummed his fingers on the desk and glanced at his watch. He shuffled papers from point A to point B. He called Toronto again at 7:30 and received an automated answering machine this time. He went out for coffee and a newspaper.

He received a busy signal on his third attempt. Finally, a woman answered. "CanChem."

"Good morning. I'm Special Agent Bill Hamilton with the Bureau of Alcohol, Tobacco and Firearms in the United States. I'm in need of information about some of your shipments to Miami, Florida."

The woman responded with a long silence.

"Hello?" Hamilton said. "You still there?"

"What specifically do you want?" she asked.

"I'm interested in a large delivery of two or three hundred five-gallon containers of acetone last July or August."

"Are you affiliated with the Drug Enforcement Administration?"

"BATF—Bureau of Alcohol, Tobacco and Firearms."

"I really cannot provide you with any information."

"Let me speak to your supervisor," the agent insisted.

He would obtain information even if he had to go through diplomatic channels. One of the most infuriating aspects of his job was having to deal with bureaucratic red tape.

"I'll have the owner call you back in a few minutes," the secretary said.

As Hamilton waited, the receptionist at the front desk buzzed him. "Telephone, Bill."

It couldn't be CanChem; he had given the secretary his direct number.

"Take a message," he said.

"The caller said it's important."

"I'm in the middle of something. I'll call back."

His private number rang minutes later. A voice said, "This is Donald Bartholomew at CanChem. I understand you're interested in some information?"

The voice sounded guarded but cooperative.

"Yes. A shipment of a large quantity of acetone to a purchaser in the Miami area."

"Sorry. We manufacture only chemical safe containers, not the chemicals."

"All right. Did you ship a large number of five-gallon hard-plastic containers to Florida within the past three months or so to a single customer? The name Can-Chem is on them."

"Hold on a second."

Hamilton heard fingers stroking a keyboard. He had the impression Mr. Bartholomew already possessed the information but was delaying for some reason.

"We recently had a similar inquiry from another agency in the U.S.," Bartholomew volunteered when he returned to the line.

"Who?"

"I've been asked not to say. They also asked me not to mention their inquiry to anyone else, but under the circumstances . . ."

"Did you have the information they wanted?"

"We shipped 250 of that particular container to a warehouse in Miami for a company called . . . uh, I have it here somewhere."

That unnecessary delay again.

"Here it is. Carib Tech Traders. We shipped them on August 26."

One week before IWDC burned. It no longer seemed a coincidence that the discarded CanChem jugs were concentrated in the Carib Tech section of the warehouse.

"Which warehouse did you ship them to?" Hamilton asked. "Was it the International Warehouse Distributing Corporation—IWDC—on 79th Street?"

He *couldn't* be so lucky. The shipment had gone to an address in south Miami, 5 miles from IWDC. How had the containers ultimately ended up full of acetone in the IWDC building?

"Who signed for the shipment?" asked the BATF agent.

"A customer by the name of . . . yes . . . Afif Yordi."

Afif. Not his mother or sister.

No sooner had Hamilton hung up with CanChem than the receptionist buzzed him again.

"Bill, it's the same man as before. He said he's from the Drug Enforcement Administration. He asked to speak to you right away."

The caller introduced himself as DEA agent Jeff Roan. His, he said, was the "other agency" in contact with CanChem. The timing of his call was no coincidence. Bartholomew had reported to him before returning Hamilton's call.

"We need to get together and have a talk about Carib Tech Traders," Roan said.

Chapter

36

Much of a fire investigator's work lies outside the glamour of inquiring into multimillion-dollar insurance fraud arsons and probing fire homicides. The average city or county fire marshal's duties require spending more time on routine matters than on detecting crimes. He or she checks businesses for code violations, conducts safety inspections, delivers fire safety lectures at local high schools and to civic groups, and determines the causes of fires that may or may not be arson.

The law has placed fire investigators and inspectors in charge of every structural fire scene until they make a determination as to cause of the fire, although they usually exercise this power only if the fire is suspicious or has caused heavy damage. Because owners and residents lose temporary control of their property, restricted from removing even their own clothing or a toothbrush without permission, fire marshals frequently go to great lengths to educate the public on the reasoning behind the law.

"When we respond to a fire, we have control of your property," says Stephen McInerny, a battalion chief of the Fort Lauderdale, Florida, fire department. "You may be advised of some things people often find quite upsetting. But there is purpose behind the seeming madness."

When the inspector arrives at a fire scene, he or she usually talks to firefighters, homeowner, and neighbors before ever entering the house. What did they see, where was the hottest fire, what color was the smoke . . . ? Once inside, the inspector snaps photographs and takes sample scrapings from walls, floor, and furniture for laboratory analysis. He searches for signs of flammable liquids and "plants" of combustible materials.

"We look for the source of the fire," McInerny continues. "There is a picture in the fire's travels. We look for 'alligatoring.' That's where the fire burns the longest and most intense and is usually where it started."

At the same time, the inspector must determine if the house is safe for a family to return to. All electricity is shut off. Toxicity from smoke and other residue is evaluated.

"Just because it isn't smoky doesn't mean it's safe," explained Fire Marshal Charles Raiken, Broward County, Florida. "Fire gases such as hydrogen sulfide, carbon monoxide, and polyvinyl chloride all have latent poison effects. We have to be in protective gear even after the fire."

Firefighters must also perform fire control damage, or "essential damage," in probing for "hidden fire." It is often difficult for a homeowner to understand why firefighters cause more damage than the blaze.

"In a seemingly simple couch fire, we have to determine if the fire extended to the ceiling," Raiken continued, "so we may have to pull the entire ceiling down—and the wall. There could be a single ember in the wall that, if allowed to emit enough heat, could reignite. If the wall is still warm, we have to rip out a portion to check damage to the bearing studs.

"Windows will be broken if ventilation is needed. Then there is the tracking of ash all over, charring, and water dripping all over. I've seen apartment fires where other units' ceilings collapsed from water."

Tom Bradford of the Hollywood, Florida, fire marshal's office ruefully shook his head on recalling the reaction of irate homeowners following a fire.

"Telling them not to recover belongings from the rubble is much easier said than done," he said. "So we'll sometimes walk through the house at their risk for whatever it is, and we will document where they took it from. People get a questioning look on their faces, but our responsibility is to make sure no fraud takes place. In the trauma of moving out of their house late at night, rarely do people sit there and say, 'Okay, fine. I understand.'"

Captain Rocky McAllister recalled the morning he arrived to look at an expensive house that had suffered a fire the previous night. He found the pudgy owner in tears as he looked over the damage to his house. His angry eyes fixed on the arriving fire investigator.

"What are you doing——coming back to finish the job?" he demanded bitterly. "Your firemen did more goddamned damage than the fire did. Look at this shit. They didn't have to knock down the whole goddamned wall."

"The fire came up inside the wall," McAllister tried to explain. "Firefighters had to get to the embers."

"What the fuck do I care about embers? I'm going to have to replace *everything.*"

"Your insurance will cover it."

"This?" he blustered, indicating an oil painting firefighters had knocked off the wall, then stomped on and soaked with water. "Do you know what *this* is? Hell, *you* wouldn't know, would you?"

"I'm an uncultured plebe," McAllister snapped back, growing testy himself.

"It's a *Matisse.* Do you know what a Matisse is?"

"Like an Elvis painting on black velvet?"

"Who can afford to insure a Matisse in Miami? Do you know what that would cost?"

"A weekend ski trip to Aspen?"

The guy stormed out of the burned hulk, hurling insults back over his shoulder. "Let me know when you get through destroying everything else," he shouted.

McAllister couldn't resist. "Say, the wrecker truck is a little late. Would you direct the driver this way if you see him?"

He withstood the temptation to tack up a sign: FIRE INVESTIGATION. KEEP OUT BY ORDER OF FIRE MARSHAL. He would probably feel the same way if it were *his* house.

Chapter

37

Miami, Florida

On the first day of November, with the IWDC case 2 months old and still unsolved, Rocky McAllister worked his way through the evening post–rush hour traffic to Jackson Memorial Hospital (JMH). Earlier, dispatch advised him he had a message from BATF agent Bill Hamilton, something about DEA and Can-Chem. He tried to return the call but Hamilton had already left for the evening.

November in south Florida is a particularly delightful time of year. Summer rains have ended, the mornings are bright and exhilarating, and the days' temperatures top out in the seventies. McAllister longed for a day of boat fishing in the Everglades. Lead and other pollution in the water made the fish mostly inedible, but they also acted like growth hormones on the big bass.

His work day was already 12 hours old when he got out of his car and strode through JMH's emergency room. Child victims always touched the fire cop. Maybe it was because he had children of his own, now teenagers, and he had witnessed many times over the years what fire could do to them.

FIRE COPS

Memories of the three children in the redbrick condo always troubled him, almost like a Vietnam flashback. He had rolled on the 4 A.M. pushout because it *sounded* suspicious. A Life Flight helicopter was picking up a woman when he arrived in a drizzling rain. Her children were still inside the condo. McAllister volunteered to accompany a rescue assault team. The condo was really going, shooting sparks into the night sky.

The rescue patrol charged into the smoke as through a living wall and into a different dimension——a dark, smoky world that seemed to be forever changing and rearranging itself, peopled by shadows and the subdued surreal beams of flashlights probing the hellish environs. All furnishings were piles of ashes out of which stuck ill-defined chars of wood and metal, springs and frames. Blackened carpet crunched beneath heavy boots. Floods shining through from outside danced ghosts through the smoke.

Signs of arson were so obvious as to strain credulity. A gas can containing residue of gasoline that had not yet burned or oxidized lay discarded on the floor, and next to it, the remains of a cigarette lighter. Signs of how the fire traveled from the *top* of the stairs to the *bottom*, something fire rarely did without an accelerant trailer assisting it, told the story as clearly as would a typed page. Spilled gasoline and its fumes went up in a startling explosion, as gasoline will, as soon as it was ignited. The fire starter panicked, dropping the gasoline can and his lighter as he——or perhaps she——bolted to safety.

The first corpse lay smoldering at the head of the stairs——a small teenage black girl. Nearby lay the charred remains of a little boy of about 5, his body drawn into a scorched ball as if he had been trying to make himself smaller and harder for the fire to find. The third victim, another little girl of 10 or so, lay curled in the bathtub.

Metro–Dade cops had a suspect in custody by the

time the rescue team emerged from the fire. A shirtless, middle-aged man slumped in the backseat cage of a black-and-white at curbside.

"Rocky, this is Nathan Powell," a police officer said. "He lived here with his wife, his 5-year-old son, and his wife's two daughters. We found him down the block acting crazy and reeking of gasoline. It didn't take a brain surgeon to figure it out."

"Powell, look at me," McAllister demanded.

"No, man. *No.*"

"Look at me. Why did you do it? *Why did you kill your kids?*"

"Man, I don't know. *I don't know.* Maybe I'm crazy, man. That's all I can figure. Crazy mad at *her,* the bitch—and she didn't even die."*

The finding of the dead children marked the beginning of McAllister's lifelong hatred of arsonists and his continually growing compassion for fire's small victims. He thought of the three little ones now as he entered a room in JMH, where a 5-year-old girl lay motionless in bed, monitored by machines and tubes running from her every orifice. Mom and Dad left her at home in the care of her 11-year-old brother while they went grocery shopping. Brother left sister at home alone while he bopped off down the street to shoot hoops with a buddy.

That was when the fire monster struck.

Aside from the fire cop's empathy for small victims, he had two other reasons for stopping by the hospital. First, his investigation demanded he know if the little girl was going to survive; dead victims placed more pressure on the inquiry. The second reason was because seeing her gave a human face to the tragedy and made him aware of more than burn patterns and smoke

---

*Nathan Powell was convicted and sentenced to life imprisonment for the murder of his son and stepdaughters.

stains on inanimate materials. *People,* not property, were the motivating force behind his job. He was much more than merely a tax-subsidized investigator for the insurance companies.

The little girl lay within a ring of soft light. She appeared tiny and frail, almost fragile. McAllister stood with hat in hand.

"Her condition is stable," a nurse assured him, standing on the other side of the bed.

"She's going to make it?"

"She'll have scars. What an awful shame that little kids must suffer."

"Yes," Rocky said. "A terrible shame."

Yellow evidence tape encircled the blackened corpse of the little girl's house on a run-down block north of downtown Miami. The wood-framed cottage had recently been painted pale blue and appeared surprisingly well kept for this neighborhood. The walls and most of the roof, although scorched, remained standing. Built-up heat inside the house during the fire had blown window glass all over the narrow lawn. The charred front door hung by one hinge.

Damage inside was more complete. Water and ashes created a black paste that covered the skeletons of a television set, a sofa burned down to springs and frame, and several other scraps of furniture. The house already smelled of mildew and abandonment. The red fading sun shining through a gaping hole where a window had been lent the dwelling the forlorn feeling that its residents had died or moved away and would never return.

If houses, like pets, assumed the characteristics of their owners, this house must have been a lively and fun-loving cocker spaniel. It seemed sad now, scorched tail pulled between its legs, head drooping.

McAllister shrugged off the depression that seemed to cloak the dead house and got to work. Although he doubted arson, the law required he investigate and report the cause of the blaze. He limbered up his Instamatic and shot frames from room to room, recording what remained of a family's life: remnants and scraps. Melted dolls and a charred toy police car. Scorched mementos and smoke-stained clothing. Certificates, documents, photographs, books, letters—the shreds of a family's identity, items that documented the family's life.

An inverted cone-shaped burn pattern etched into the wall behind the TV revealed the origin of the fire. The investigator squatted as he studied charred electrical cords converging on the fire source in fragmented segments. Four cords led to a TV, a VCR, a lamp, and a Nintendo game, respectively. Nothing as insidious as faulty wiring, a lightning strike, or errant behavior started the fire. It ignited when an overloaded electrical outlet sparked a blaze in the wall.

McAllister used a flashlight as he took notes for his report. He was so engrossed in his work that the stealthy intrusion of a footfall startled him. He sprang to his feet and spun around in the darkened room. Thieves often monitored emergency radios in order to find fire-damaged houses to loot.

His eyes scanned corners and doorways—and saw nothing. Eerie damned places, the burned skeletons of houses after sunset.

"Hello?"

No answer. He returned to his work.

Scurrying sounds from another room and a passing body knocked something over. It fell with a crash.

Rocky charged to the bedroom. Nothing there either. He hesitated, unsure.

He went from room to room, searching with his flashlight. Two glowing eyes suddenly peered at him from underneath what had once been the dining-room table. He froze, then chuckled with self-conscious relief, glad Fuhrman had not witnessed this little episode. He dropped to one knee.

"Here, kitty, kitty . . . come here, kitty. What happened to you? Where did everybody go?"

He picked up the kitten, intending to drop it off at the motel where the Red Cross had lodged the displaced family. The little girl would be pleased to know her pet was okay when she regained consciousness. He dialed his home number on his cell phone as he pulled into traffic.

"Honey," he said when Nancy answered. "I'm going to be a little late for dinner."

"I'm not surprised. How's your day been?"

"Typical day. If Bill Hamilton calls, tell him I'll phone him as soon as I get home."

Chapter

38

Miami, Florida

DEA agents Jeff Harrison and A. B. Duquette seemed embarrassed that Afif Yordi and his cousin Kamal Jurdi had somehow slipped away from their house with 250 5-gallon containers full of highly volatile acetone and apparently delivered it to the IWDC warehouse *while they were under surveillance*. Harrison scowled and Duquette sucked on his ever-present cigarette. They, along with BATF's Bill Hamilton, Detective Wil Fuhrman, Captain Rocky McAllister, and DEA supervisor Jeff Roan were stuffed into Roan's office.

"We knew nothing about the fire or Yordi's being the subject of another criminal investigation until Can-Chem informed us about your inquiry," Roan explained. "We were onto what we thought to be a coke lab."

Roan summarized the details. Afif Yordi, operating as Carib Tech Traders, used his credit cards to rent trucks from the Ryder offices at 3001 Northwest 87th Avenue, eight blocks from the IWDC warehouse. He used his first rental 2 weeks before the fire to purchase 25 55-gallon drums of acetone from a corporation in Opa Locka, Florida. That was the transaction that instigated DEA interest. Surveillance was immediately placed on Yordi's residence in an attempt to locate the drug lab to which the acetone was presumably delivered.

The following week, Yordi rented another Ryder and picked up 250 jugs from a south Miami warehouse, where they had been delivered by CanChem.

"We traced CanChem to Toronto the same way you did," Roan informed the fire cops. "Yordi purchased the canisters under the business name of Carib Tech Traders. It wasn't like he attempted to cover his tracks or anything."

By September 2, DEA agents had settled in on the Yordi residence instead of tailing Yordi and Jurdi all over Miami. They were convinced the drug lab was located inside the residence and were working to obtain sufficient probable cause for a search warrant. For that reason, no agent picked up the trails of either the Ryder or the white van when each left the residence separately during the afternoon of that date. Kamal Jurdi drove the Ryder; Yordi, the white van. Jurdi returned the rental truck at 6:12 P.M. Agents subsequently scoured the returned truck for signs of cocaine, finding nothing.

Two hours later, at 8:30 P.M., a Metro–Dade police detective named Andrus was working an off-duty job guarding warehouses when he spotted a white Ford step van nosing around the area. More diligent than the rookie cop who observed the hab in the area the same night, the detective pulled the van over near Northwest 84th Avenue and 12th Street, six blocks northwest of the IWDC warehouse. The driver appeared alone in the vehicle.

Andrus jotted down the van's tag number—Florida 945-ARZ. It turned out to be the same van under surveillance by DEA agents. The operator politely produced a driver's license in the name of Kamal Jurdi. He was a wiry, dark-complexioned man in his early thirties. A partition behind the seats blocked off a view of the cargo area. The detective noticed some papers lying on the vacant passenger's seat. A citizens band (CB) radio was turned on.

"Anything wrong, officer?" Kamal Jurdi asked with a smile.

"What are you doing?" Andrus asked. "There are no businesses open in here this time of night."

Nothing about the driver's demeanor prompted the police officer's suspicions. He displayed no symptoms of nervousness as he explained, "I was passing by on my way home. I remembered I needed to be at an address the first thing in the morning. I thought I'd find it and drive by tonight so I wouldn't have to hunt for it in the morning."

Sounded reasonable. The officer ran a radio R&W— records and wanted—on the man's name. He came back clean.

"Did you find your address?" Andrus asked him, returning his license.

"I think it's just ahead. I'll drive by to make sure."

The van lurched into gear and eased slowly away. Andrus followed until it turned into the parking lot of a warehouse. Jurdi waved. Was it merely coincidence that the parking lot in which he turned around belonged to IWDC?

On September 8, after another 6 days of shadowing the suspects' house, during which time neither Yordi nor Jurdi were seen, DEA struck with an early morning search warrant. Yordi's mother Nayat answered the door, her little Pekingese face squeezed into a scowl.

"We have a search warrant," Harrison said. "Do you understand? We have to come in. How many people are inside the house?"

"One other person only. My daughter Najua."

Harrison gently pushed her aside. Najua stood behind her mother, nervously clasping a nightgown around her throat.

"The house was clean—*clean*," Duquette informed

the fire cops. "No acetone, no CanChem jugs, no coke. Nothing. It had all disappeared. So had Afif and his cousin. They were supposedly 'out of town on business, please.' We haven't been able to locate them since. I'll admit it looks like they sneaked acetone out on us that ended up in your warehouse fire."

"That little bastard Afif was probably already inside the warehouse when Andrus stopped Jurdi," Wil Fuhrman grumbled, "along with twelve hundred fifty gallons of acetone and a two-way radio in contact with his cousin's CB."

But how did he get the acetone inside without forcing entry and setting off the burglar alarm?

"That's hard to figure," Fuhrman admitted. "Apparently, both subjects bugged out somewhere after the fire. You haven't seen them again and we can't find them. They didn't socialize with many folks, so we pretty much have to take Mama's word that they're overseas. So far, no insurance claims have been filed—and we still can't prove intent to defraud. Possession of acetone in itself is not a crime. You'd have thought that with a half-million dollars at stake, the Yordis would be camped out waiting for the insurance claims office to pay off."

Chapter

39

Sapulpa, Oklahoma

Everyone in the tract house on North Gary Place in Tulsa—little ticky-tacky boxes all in a row—appeared asleep at 9:30 A.M. on October 12, 6 days after Laura Lee Sanders and Michael Houghton were baked alive in Laura's Cutlass. Tulsa uniformed officers, led by 25-year veteran Walt Milner, slid their black-and-whites silently into place at either end of the block. Other officers stole through yards from behind to thwart escape in that direction.

The manhunt for murder-rape suspects Robert Wayne Lambert and his teenage sidekick Scott Allen Hain had taken a frenetic pace after October 8 when Sergeant Buck Gardner jumped the pair in Houghton's stolen Isuzu pickup. Detective Bruce Duncan in Sapulpa and his counterpart, Steve Steele, in Tulsa, continued to accumulate evidence against the young killers, who, thus far, had eluded capture.

On October 10, a snitch being worked by Tulsa Detective Mike Huff had requested a confidential meet. Not only did the informant know Lambert and Hain, he actually *saw* them the previous Thursday night following their wild car chase escape from the police. They hid out at the snitch's apartment in the government-subsidized projects on West Maybelle Street, a notorious nest of dopers and thieves.

"They were sweating and out of breath from running," the snitch said. "They said the cops were chasing them. They said it was because they robbed and burned that man and woman in Sapulpa."

Huff and his partner Mike Cook, an ex–Air Force fighter pilot turned cop, took the one lead and traced the killers to North Gary Place in Tulsa, where Scott Hain had lived on and off with relatives before being jailed in "kiddie prison." By secretly questioning neighbors, the cops learned that Hain had been seen at the residence as recently as the weekend. One man had noticed a blue Isuzu pickup at the house last Monday or Tuesday.

"We haven't seen either of them. We don't know where they are," residents at the targeted house told Huff and all but slammed the door in his face.

"We know they're lying, covering up for Hain," Huff reported to Steele.

Huff and Cook went quietly from house to house in the neighborhood, asking neighbors to keep an eye on the Hain house.

"If you should see Lambert or Hain, we'd appreciate a tipoff. You don't even have to give your name when you call," Huff assured his recruits.

That anonymous call had popped into the Tulsa dispatcher's office on the morning of October 12.

"Okay. I've seen a couple of guys going in and out of the garage over there. I think one of 'em is Scott Hain. It looks like they're hiding out."

Trotting close in front of the houses on the block to prevent premature discovery, Officer Walt Milner spotted the garage in question. It was slightly behind and to the side of the house, detached from it. A cracked concrete drive led past a giant oak to the garage. All seemed peaceful and normal as Milner worked his way toward the structure using the oak as cover. He saw other "green shirts"—so called because of the color of their uniforms—draw their weapons as they approached from behind. He drew his.

Hain and Lambert came packaged with their own warning label: CONSIDER ARMED AND DANGEROUS.

Nearly 20 years earlier, Milner's own daughter, only 10 years old, had been the victim of one of the most heinous and infamous crimes in Oklahoma history. She and her two little tent mates had been raped and bludgeoned to death on their first night of Girl Scout summer camp at Camp Scott near Pryor. Milner often seemed driven after that to put as many criminals in jail as he could.

Green shirts surrounded the garage and house. Still using the tree as cover, Milner shouted, "Hain! Lambert! This is the police. You are under arrest. Come on out with your hands up."

He paused, then added in a sterner addendum: "You don't *want* us to come in and get you."

Monday silence prevailed for long minutes. It seemed this might be another false alarm. But, then, detectives' efforts in grooming the neighborhood paid off. The garage door opened. Out came Scott Allen Hain with his hands in the air. Another slender young man with scraggly blond hair followed him in the same posture. Both wore sullen, resigned expressions. But both, Milner noted, were "as meek as lambs."

"Are you Hain?" Milner asked the youngest. Long hair fell across the youth's face. He nodded.

"And you're Lambert?"

"No. I'm Johnny Tolbert."

"That's funny," Sgt. Steve Steele remarked when the two were delivered to him at the downtown police station in handcuffs. He displayed a mug shot of Robert Wayne Lambert. "You look exactly like this guy in the picture."

The blond man stared. Then he folded, slumping

where he stood. His next words poured out in a nervous rush: "I stole the car, but I didn't kill nobody."

That was all it took. Seasoned detectives know that once the slightest inroad is made into a suspect's psyche, they own him. He will "spill his guts" after that. He will tell everything without regard to old loyalties and friendships. All he craves is the chance to alleviate his own guilt and lay it on someone else.

"I can hardly wait to hear *this* confession," Steele confided in a wry aside to other officers.

Chapter

40

According to Arnold Madison, who conducted a study of fire starters detailed in his book *Arson,* teenage arsonists like Scott Allen Hain exhibit behavior that fits a pattern of "character disorder" begun in childhood. They often have histories of unhappy homes, drug and alcohol abuse, and poor attendance at school and express unreasonable anger against society.

"Whether hidden or broadcast," he explained, "it is this fury that causes them to set fires. If they are angry with their parents, their own home may be set afire. Anger at school officials results in school arson. Or the revenge may be directed at the 'establishment' or society in general."

"But it is not 'society in general' that suffers most from these characters, teenagers or not," counters Tulsa Detective Steve Steele. "It wasn't 'society' Hain and Lambert stuffed into the truck of that car and burned. They had names. They were *people.*"

Madison claims that it was one such expression of anger that resulted in more than 1,000 fires being set by teenagers and adults over a 36-hour period during the infamous New York City blackout in 1977. Three people were killed and 59 firefighters injured.

However, while "fury" may or may not underlie the motivation behind the high incidence of teenage arson, it is quite clear that few teenage pyros are motivated by financial profit, which is a primary motive for adult arson fires. For most teens, excluding the truly vicious and disturbed ones, setting fires provides "fun" or relief from boredom. "Joke" fires in rural and suburban areas, like false alarms in the cities, are viewed as harmless pranks.

Psychiatrists are not certain why teens turn to arson alone or arson in relation to other crimes. Some believe that it is because the tools needed to start a fire are easy to obtain or because some youngsters crave media attention. Others suspect that it is because they discover the awesome power of fire at an early age and are thrilled at fire's potential for enormous havoc for only a small investment in time and energy. The world takes notice when something burns!

Chapter

41

Sapulpa, Oklahoma

While 17-year-old Scott Hain remained "on ice" in another room, 21-year-old Bobby Lambert detailed for Detectives Steele and Duncan the gruesome events of the morning of October 6. Interrupting his confession for periodic bouts of sobbing and sniffling—*Don't anyone feel sorry for me for getting caught?*—he explained how he and Hain had started out the night planning to rob a house in Tulsa's Brookside area. Instead, they spotted a young man and woman sitting in a car in the darkness of a tavern parking lot. They decided it would be easier to rob the couple than to break into a house.

Lambert, armed with a BB-pellet pistol, and Hain, armed with a knife, crawled on their bellies up beside the car in the darkness and sprang upon the unsuspecting couple. Lambert forced the young woman to drive. Hain, in the back seat with Houghton, held a knife to the hostage's throat. They circled the block once in Laura Lee's Cutlass before learning of Houghton's truck. They returned to the parking lot. It was late, after 2 A.M., so the lot was deserted.

After robbing the couple of nearly $400 in cash,

Lambert tied Houghton's hands and feet and forced him into the trunk of Laura's car. The woman was left unbound but likewise was forced into the trunk and the lid slammed.

The ex-con took the lead in the Isuzu pickup; Hain followed, driving the Oldsmobile with the hapless man and woman locked in the trunk. They could be heard whispering in frightened tones.

Lambert turned into an isolated Sapulpa field near where he used to live with his mother. There, both assailants undoubtedly raped Laura Lee, although both denied it. Afterward, Lambert cut the car's fuel line to let gasoline run out.

He sobbed in the interrogation room, "I couldn't do it. I told Scott, 'I can't do it.' I started walking back to the truck. Scott lit it up. I turned around and the car was on fire. They were hollering. I ran back and tried to put out the fire with a blanket—but I couldn't."

Sure you did, you murdering bastard, Steele thought. It was so typical of killers after they were caught to try to mitigate their acts.

Lambert backed off from the blaze, he said, and listened to the screams of the two Tulsans as they burned to death. Then he and Hain left to go cop some marijuana with their loot.

The killers' travels over the following 2 days in the stolen Isuzu truck took them to a friend's house in Jennings and then on to Wichita, where they stayed until their return to Tulsa. They didn't bother to switch license plates on the hot truck.

"They were vicious," Steele commented to Duncan, "but no one could ever accuse them of being smart."

Steele took the videotape of Lambert's confession with him into Scott Hain's interrogation. Hain still pouted. He looked up from where he slumped, arms on knees.

"I don't know what this is all about," he claimed. "I ain't had nothing to do with any of this."

Steele shrugged. "No? Bobby said *you* were the one who lit the car up."

"I don't believe it."

The detective jerked a thumb at a TV monitor. "Wanna watch?" he asked. He played the weeping drama of Bobby Wayne Lambert's unbosoming. A new state law permitted police to question juveniles between the ages of 16 and 18 suspected of committing certain high classes of felonies.

Hain stared at the monitor, gulping. After a while, he could no longer remain silent.

"That ain't the way it was!" he suddenly bellowed.

"How was it, then?" Detective Duncan prompted.

In Scott Hain's own videotaped confession, he remained controlled and without emotion, in stark contrast to his older partner's choking and lamenting. Lambert, he insisted, was the torch. *He* was the one who cut the car's fuel line, stuffed a gasoline-saturated blanket and newspaper under the steering column, then struck a match.

"They were hollering, but you couldn't understand what they were saying," Hain said without change of expression. "You could hear scuffling sounds in the trunk, banging."

The two arsonists stood and watched the car burn for several minutes, until the screams subsided. Then they got into Houghton's pickup. Before they drove away, they stopped once more to make sure the Cutlass was burning properly.*

---

*Scott Allen Hain and Robert Wayne Lambert were each found guilty of arson homicide and robbery and sentenced to the death penalty. Currently on death row, they also face criminal charges in Oklahoma and Kansas for other crimes of rape, assault, and robbery associated with their 3-month serial-crime spree.

Chapter

42

Miami, Florida

Bill Hamilton grinned wryly, concentrating in the mirror while he clumsily made a Windsor knot in his tie. Sharp features tanned from life in the Florida sunshine reflected back at him. He still looked fit, like the former Marine he was in Vietnam. He finished the knot and adjusted his tie. He rarely wore the damned things anymore. Not much call for them in the blackened centers of gutted buildings.

"Tell me again who's having this Christmas party?" he pleaded of his wife Bonnie, who was giving last-minute instructions to 14-year-old daughter Elizabeth on baby-sitting 11-year-old——"Don't call it *baby-sitting!*"——Justin.

"Stop it, honey. You know darn well Pamela is my oldest friend."

Hamilton was a private man not much disposed to large gatherings. Often being the only law-enforcement officer present put him even more at unease. Some guy always found out he was a BATF agent and cornered him. It started with the dark jokes.

Guess who just stopped smokin'?
David Koresh.

Know how to pick up Branch Davidian chicks?
Dustbuster.

What were God's first words to David Koresh when
he arrived in heaven?
"Well done."

Although Hamilton had not been directly involved in the Waco standoff, it affected him and every other BATF agent in a very personal way. Wherever agents were identified in public, they were automatically associated with the fiery disaster on the Texas plains that claimed the lives of religious fanatic David Koresh and his followers. It was like the public held each agent *personally* responsible, however removed he or she might have been from the event. Someone invariably remarked, "The BATF and the government really screwed up there."

Chapter

43

Waco, Texas

Inarguably, it was one of the most notorious cases of self-immolating arson in U.S. history. At the peak of the fire at noon, April 19, 1993, temperatures inside the roiling ball of orange flame that took down David Koresh and the Branch Davidian compound on the Texas flats near Waco reached 2,000 degrees. Bodies were cremated at those temperatures. Only skulls and rib cages remained in many instances. There wasn't enough left of some people, especially the children, to fill a coffee cup. Some of the 81 people who perished in the blaze, including 25 children, were never found.

The compound had been turned into rubble, with only remnants of human habitation——a metal kitchen pantry twisted like a charred skeleton, oxidized bed-springs beneath the ashes and debris from the collapsed roof, exploded fruit and vegetable cans with the labels blackened off, remains of metal fittings and electrical fixtures and buckets and false teeth . . .

The fire only lasted 20 minutes, but it continued to smoke for a week. John Cabaniss, McLennon County justice of the peace, had the grimly ironic task of declaring the bits of bodies and ashes officially deceased. Tarrant County medical examiner Nizam Peerwani attempted to identify the remains.

Cabaniss and fire investigators from both McLennon County and Tarrant County rummaged amidst the debris of the destruction, looking for pieces of bodies. They erected a tiny orange flag over each recognizable piece of human remains. The flags grew slowly into a grisly field of carrion flowers.

The BATF operation that was supposed to arrest David Koresh for weapons violations was called Operation Trojan Horse. Three cattle trucks covered with tarps and containing armed agents were the Trojan horses. Three military-type helicopters buzzed overhead. The news media filmed it all from the road a half mile away.

It was supposed to be a surprise raid.

Waco Tribune-Herald *reporter Mark England watched the helicopters circling on the horizon for several minutes before the raid commenced. "As the cattle trucks swung up a long dirt road in front of the compound, the helicopters came in low from the north. a Blackhawk helicopter hovering like an angry wasp over the rambling building. Agents wearing blue jumpsuits and flak jackets leaped out of the cattle trucks, throwing concussion grenades and screaming, "Come out!"*

Firing and confusion began immediately.

Concussion grenades exploded all over the compound. Agents threw ladders against the wooden building believed to contain the Branch Davidian armory. Officers scurried up the ladders to the roof adjacent to the armory.

The defenders were armed with M16 assault rifles and several .50-caliber machine guns. A deadly hail of gunfire poured from the compound. It scythed through the attackers, cutting them down. An agent used a crowbar to smash out the armory window. Three agents disappeared through it.

Gunfire had already been coming out of the window. Bullets punctured the roof around the agents and the walls in front of them, blowing wood fragments high into the air. An agent on the roof convulsed as at least one bullet struck him. He hobbled to the ladder and slid to the ground.

Bill Buford and Robb Williams were two of the agents assigned to penetrate the armory. As they entered through the smashed window, the walls around them erupted in bullets and splinters. Buford took several chunks of lead in the leg and one in the hip before he managed to get out again. He collapsed and rolled off the roof, breaking several ribs, then was hit again while he lay on the ground.

He saw Robb Williams killed.

Williams had crouched behind an abandoned safe. Hit in the shoulder, he fell backward. He got back up, still firing. A second bullet drove through his helmet. He did not get up that time.

Agent Steven Willis leaped out of one of the cattle trucks. A rifleman lying atop the water tower killed him. An agent from across the road shot the sniper off the tower. He fell 30 feet and his body lay there, slowly rotting, for several days.

The withering, deafening firefight—a flashback for some of the Vietnam veterans, such as Bill Buford—continued uninterrupted for 45 minutes, then sporadically for another hour after that. BATF officers took cover behind anything available and returned fire. Thousands of rounds were exchanged.

At the end of the day, four BATF agents had been killed in action—Robb Williams, Conway LeBleu, Steve Willis, and Todd McKeehan. Fifteen more were wounded. Five Davidians were known to be killed. They were carried into Koresh's subterranean chambers, where their bodies lay putrefying and the flesh melted off the skulls.

February 28: the siege began.

During his nearly 40 years' tenure as justice of the peace, John Cabaniss had become familiar with death, inured to its presence. "I can go see a body in a field that is rising and falling with maggots and still eat rice for supper."

But this awful place, with its odors of rotted and barbecued flesh, touched him: a mother clutching a fire-gutted black object that used to be her child; bodies curled in on themselves, warped and carbonized and buckled by the heat.

"Here is the blackness and the grayness of an area that once was life, and now, it's just rubble. And yet it's all surrounded by the beautiful rolling countryside. And you think of the beauty of all those children who are dead, some of them in the ashes around you there, who at one time were playing and laughing and looking out at that lake, the rolling hills, the greenness of life— and there's nothing here anymore but the grayness and blackness of death . . .

"It was almost like a physical presence. I'm not talking about angels or demons or spirits flying around, but the awful, awesome presence of many deaths. That is almost like an entity in itself. It's an awe of the reality of death, I guess you'd have to say.

"It doesn't stay with you the whole time you're out there. You get hot, you get tired, the smoke is still coming out of the place there. A can of food blows up and you damn near jump out of your hide. But it keeps coming back to you—that awful presence of many dead people."

After the shootout, BATF wanted to assure Koresh publicly that he and his followers could still come out without being harmed. Agent leaders contacted KRLD radio in Dallas to broadcast those assurances. Koresh telephoned KRLD and did a live interview.

"I've been shot. I'm bleeding bad," he said. A baby

howled in the background. "I'm going home. I'm going back to my Father. Your weapons have overcome me this time. I begged these men to go away. . . . There are a lot of children here. . . . A two-year-old child— my daughter—has been killed. . . ."

He said he would not come out, could not come out, until he finished writing what he called his Book of the Seven Seals. *"My Father, my God who sits on the throne in heaven, has given me a book of seven seals. . . . The mystery of God is to be finished as God has declared to His servants, the prophets. . . . My reward, which is the books, is with me to give unto every man the knowledge of the seven seals. . . ."*

BATF called in hundreds of officers from the FBI and the Texas Department of Public Safety. Bradley fighting vehicles moved in the next morning, followed by larger and virtually invulnerable U.S. Army M1-Abrams tanks.

"I have a hard time seeing Koresh giving up," an acquaintance of the Davidian leader confided to news reporter Mark England. "I think he'll grow so weak (from his wound) that he knows he doesn't have much time left or he'll believe they're going to storm the place. Then, I think he'll go out in a blaze of glory."

Medical examiners, detectives, and arson and forensics experts morbidly sifted their way, inch by inch, through the ashes. The corpses were all but inseparable, bones and charred flesh melded and twisted into each other. Scorched masses of humanity had to be pried apart. Then they were shipped to Fort Worth, Texas, to be further separated, autopsied, catalogued and, perhaps, identified.

Davidians began killing themselves after the fire started. Perhaps they shot each other as part of a pact—or perhaps they committed suicide out of desperation because they could not escape. Whatever the motive, many of them mercifully killed others and themselves before the fire did it for them.

David Koresh also took the easy way out: either he shot himself or someone else did it for him. When his body, bearing a death grin, was finally identified, there was a bullet hole in the center of his skull.

The siege dragged on for 51 days, from the last of winter into spring. The road outside the compound became a circus, lined with tanks, news vans, tractors, tents, barbecue and cold-drink stands, and vendors of T-shirts, hats, postcards, and photos of David Koresh. It cost $1 to look at the silent compound through a small telescope or a pair of binoculars. There were psychics, and eccentrics, and at least five prophets, one God, three stuttering Jesus Christs, and an old man wearing an IT'S NEVER TOO LATE TO HAVE A HAPPY SECOND CHILDHOOD hat.

Government troops hung high-voltage lights and at night turned the compound into a blaze of light. They also wired up giant loudspeakers and used them to deprive the Davidians of peace by day and sleep by night. They played roaring recordings of dial tones, screaming rabbits, Buddhist chants, Christmas carols and Alice Cooper songs. The sounds and the lights were used as punishments (and their absence, as rewards) to entice Koresh to lead his people out and into captivity.

"I don't understand the negotiators," said one observer. "They try to get them to come out by offering food and freedom and telling them, 'When you come out you can tell the story. Just come on out; we won't do you any harm.' But then what they see is those Bradleys running around and the guys in them shooting the finger at these kids, and one incident where they actually mooned some of the girls. These people are scared. The only thing they see is a bunch of people coming and shooting at them."

And Representative John Conyers of Michigan de-

manded of Attorney General Janet Reno: "When in God's name is law enforcement at the federal level going to understand that these are very sensitive events—that you can't put barbed wire, guns, FBI, and Secret Service around them, send in sound 24 hours of the day and night, and then wonder why they do something unstable?"

John Cabaniss said, "The thing that preoccupied me about this level mass of awful debris is that underneath it, just a few days ago, there was some kind of habitation for living beings, with food and places where they ate and slept and talked to each other, no matter what their crazy ideas. They were about a type of life that bound them to their leader in such a way that they would follow him to death."

Dr. Phil Arnold, Ph.D., conducted a live interview with David Koresh via telephone for a Christian radio station. He argued that David could write his book on the Seven Seals while in prison. All the great prophets like Jeremiah, Moses, and Jesus had faced their accusers and gone to prison.

"We suggested that he could do it after he surrendered," Arnold explained, "that he could go to prison and write it there. But . . . he feared he would be killed in prison. He decided to write it before he surrendered, to be safe."

The FBI's patience wore thin. On April 8, the FBI announced through its daily news briefing that Koresh must come out soon.

"We're going to have to regroup," said a spokesman, "and we'll have to decide what other measures we can take. There are other weapons in our arsenal."

Clouds of flies swarmed over the decomposing burned flesh. Cabaniss wondered about the last moments: "I don't know for sure, but I've heard that they injected (the children) with something and that they probably died before the fire. I don't know if someone just made it up, but it's a nice thought. . . . I hope they had something so that they didn't have to realize the horror of a fiery death."

April 19, day 51 of the siege, 6:05 A.M. A huge tanklike M-60 combat engineering vehicle with a special boom attached to it lumbered up and started punching a hole into the main building of the compound. It blew tear gas into the building while choppers whumped-whumped *overhead and FBI snipers peered through their scopes. Some Davidians shot at the armored vehicle, but the feds did not return fire.*

Loudspeakers boomed: "This is not an assault. If you fire, we will return fire. We are introducing nonlethal tear gas. Exit the compound and follow instructions. Come out and you will not be harmed. No one will be injured. Do not subject yourself to any further discomfort. Submit to the proper authorities. . . ."

Jeffrey Jamar was the FBI agent in charge. He and others viewed the compound through binoculars and listened over eavesdropping devices that had previously been delivered with food and water. They overheard someone shout, "Don't shoot until the very last minute." Another voice ordered, "Stay low. Stay ready and loaded."

The defenders, Jamar said, "were very disciplined, putting their masks on and gathering in a central area where the effects of the gas were limited."

The battering and gassing by the combat vehicles continued until 9 A.M., and then there was a 2½-hour lull. A spokesperson for the FBI explained the action to the press. "The action taken today was the next logical step in a series of actions to bring this episode to a conclusion. . . . We will continue to gas, probably all of today. . . . At this point, we're not negotiating. We're saying, 'Come out with your hands up. This matter is over.'"

AT 11:30 A.M., the M-60s resumed battering and gassing. One machine took out an 8-foot chunk of wall as it crashed through the compound's front door.

The FBI spokesman said, "Is suicide a possibility? We thought that this was probably the best way to prevent that type of suicide pact from taking place—to cause confusion inside the compound. We hoped that their motherly instincts would take over and that they would want their children out of that environment."

Government snipers watching through their scopes saw a figure inside the compound light a rag or paper and throw it down. Flames burst from that point, and then from two other points as the cultists ignited their own funeral pyre.

The pale wafting smoke rising from the tear gas turned into a white and yellow cloud. Smoke then billowed darker and wider, turning black and rising, swirling in a tethered tornado of fury. The first bloom of bright flame sprouted in the center of the tornado— and then David Koresh's prophecy of hell on earth came true.

The second floor burned away, collapsing into the first. Then the walls of the first floor listed, swayed, and crumpled into the fire. Twelve of the 25 children died wrapped in the arms of their mothers.

Chapter

44

Miami, Florida

Within days after the IWDC fire, insurance companies had begun paying off clients' losses. By January, all claims, with the exception of two, had been settled. Those two belonged to the owner, Rami Rabjami, who had been greatly underinsured and had to wait on the outcome of the investigation to settle and declare bankruptcy, and to Carib Tech Traders.

A Pillsbury Doughboy–type loan officer at Afif Yordi's insurance company blinked in surprise when Detective Fuhrman asked if the Yordis had yet made a claim.

"A fire? One of our local clients suffered a recent fire loss? When was that?"

"September third. Carib Tech Traders."

"No claims have been filed by Mr. Yordi."

Yordi was too hot to carry out the intended fraud of the insurance company, Fuhrman reflected, no pun intended. *If* Yordi were still alive, he must know the feds were onto his ass.

Hours of painstaking attention to detail in reconstructing Carib Tech cargo revealed that high-quality, very expensive VCRs and other electronic marvels from Singapore and China listed on bills of lading did not, in fact, exist. All that had been in the warehouse were the *cabinets* of these items.

"The *real* value of Carib Tech merchandise destroyed in the fire was how much?" McAllister asked Bill Hamilton.

"Carib Tech listed the value of the audiovisual deluxe cabinets at eighty-five dollars each without the electronics. We've found you can buy the identical cabinet at any discount store for less than twenty dollars each. No audiovisual equipment had been installed in the cabinets."

"So, the total value of actual loss?"

"A ball-park figure? Say twenty thousand dollars, plus or minus a dollar or two."

A $600,000 insurance policy on goods worth no more than $20,000. Still . . .

"We can't prove motive for arson, yet, unless someone benefits or attempts to benefit from it," Hamilton concluded wearily.

Yordi had used customs documents to verify his cargo's value in extending his insurance coverage. That meant some official along the export route must either have been bribed or have otherwise participated in the apparent fraud conspiracy in order to pass grandly inflated cargo into the United States.

"We are able to trace the cargo through the steamship line from Taiwan to its disembarkation in Miami," an official at the U.S. State Department informed Hamilton. "U.S. Customs checked the bills without physically looking at the merchandise. However, customs fees on the declared value of $417,000 *were* paid. The paper trail shows nothing was taken from the cargo or added to it from Taiwan until it was delivered to the IWDC warehouse. Presumably, contents were checked and verified at the point of export."

Would State assist in the international investigation?

"The reality of it," said the bureaucrat, "is that we

could expend manpower and money trying to trace responsibility to the individual who permitted the inflated value of the merchandise, but in the end, we'd probably know little more than we know now. Asia has a particular way of playing loose with the rules. The import–export business is rife with cheating and evading the laws of the United States and other countries. People protect each other in the government. We know from experience that they'll refuse to cooperate.

"In most of Asia, there's a thin line between government and private industry. Their government is not going to aid in the investigation of a crime relevant only to the U.S. I can tell you this too: the United States is not going to pick it up either. It's not in our national interest to foment discourse with trader nations, not even for the sake of a high-profile investigation into illegal imports and arson."

The bottom line, openly declared: the U.S. government refused to expend effort into tracking Afif Yordi's suspected criminal dealings out of country. Fire cops had to either make the case against him in Miami—or admit defeat and let arsonists go free.

As the investigation refocused upon the motive of insurance fraud, the cocaine connection was pushed into the background. Nothing thus far indicated that the warehouse had operated a coke-processing lab off-hours or that an accident might have initiated the explosion. Of one fact, however, fire investigators were certain: the arson had been well planned. No fire starter employed 1,250 gallons of accelerant without working out options for conveying it clandestinely into the target building, for gaining entry in order to ignite the blaze or set the timer, and for escaping safely and undetected.

Rami Rabjami insisted no acetone had been *stored* at the facility, that he would not have permitted it. DEA agents helped narrow the time window of the delivery.

On the day before the nighttime fire, they had observed unusual activity at the Yordi residence with the Ryder rental and the white van. They later concluded that the acetone disappeared from Yordi's garage on that date.

Hamilton and the BATF lab in Atlanta identified charred remnants from packing crates in the vicinity of the Carib Tech spaces within the warehouse. With the date the acetone entered the warehouse confined to September 2, the BATF response team once more examined those scorched and water-damaged files that survived the fire. It was slow going.

"Trucks are always making deliveries, coming and going," Rabjami explained.

"On the day of the fire—*the day of the fire,*" Hamilton stressed, "were there any deliveries to Carib Tech? Any kind of delivery?"

Finally, Rabjami and federal auditors produced a handful of damaged documents confirming some deliveries made on September 2. There *had* been one delivery to Carib Tech—a large one, crated and padded. It had not been marked as coming through customs, which meant it was a shipment from within U.S. borders. Its contents were not noted. Neither dock supervisors nor workers recalled the vehicle or truckers who delivered it. The source of the delivery was omitted from surviving records.

"That's how the acetone got inside," McAllister said. "Now, how did the arsonist get past the burglar alarms?"

Chapter

45

Fire passes through three stages in burning: the initial or incipient phase, the free-burning phase, and the smoldering phase.

During the incipient phase, when the fire first begins, the base temperature of the fledgling fire is about 400 degrees to 800 degrees Fahrenheit, while the room retains its normal temperature. As heat rises from the fire, it mixes with the surrounding air, warming it while at the same time being cooled by it. Pyrolysis—the process of heat being applied to a solid fuel to consume it—produces mainly water vapors and carbon dioxide at this phase. Ceiling temperatures reach about 200 degrees Fahrenheit.

If the fire is not discovered and extinguished at this phase, it continues to build up heat and the pyrolytic process accelerates. A thermal column develops and heat rises and builds up at the ceiling. Base temperatures reach 800 to 1,000 degrees Fahrenheit; ceiling temperatures at this point exceed base temperatures by as much as 600 degrees. Walls and any other flammables within the immediate vicinity begin to char and break down as flames work into them and spread, fanning out, causing the characteristic V or inverted-cone patterns to appear on any remaining walls.

It is during the free-burning that the fire reaches its maximum heat—temperatures above 2,000 degrees Fahrenheit—and causes the most destruction. Heat concentrates against the ceiling directly above the thermal column, gradually heating combustibles to their ignition temperatures. It is then that flashover occurs as the superheated fuels explode into flames.

The blaze spreads quickly during the free-burning phase, racing from room to room, igniting fuels farther and farther away from the source. Since the fire in the original area continues to burn, destroying more and more of its structure and contents, this area is usually identifiable by deep charring and near total destruction. This is the area of origin that marks where the fire began. It is the first place a fire cop looks for in starting an investigation.

Once oxygen has been consumed by the fire and drops below 13% by volume, it can no longer support flames. The fire eases back in size and temperature. It begins the smoldering phase. The thermal column disappears, replaced by heat in layers. Temperatures fall to about 1,000 degrees to 1,300 degrees Fahrenheit at the ceiling. Gases build up, especially deadly carbon monoxide, which eventually smothers the fire unless more oxygen is introduced.

Carbon monoxide has an ignition temperature of approximately 1,125 degrees Fahrenheit. Should oxygen suddenly be reintroduced into the smoldering fire—a door or window opened—superheated coals may suddenly flare, immediately raising temperatures to ignite the built-up carbon monoxide, causing a tremendous explosion. Such backdrafts have caused death or injury to many firefighters.

Then the fire has reentered immediately a free-burning phase.

A fire is killed in one or a combination of three ways: deprive it of oxygen, remove its fuel, or cool the flames below ignition point.

Chapter

46

Live Oak, Florida

The Suwannee County sheriff's office contacted the Bureau of Fire and Arson Investigation in Tallahassee early that Wednesday morning, April 25. Fire cop Ike Anderson took Interstate 10 to the Live Oak exit, then drove south through Spanish-moss country to a wide meadow in the southern part of the county. He turned his car into a pair of dry ruts and found the site of the fire an hour after he had been called away from breakfast.

Firefighters from Live Oak stood around in the meadow, still in turnouts, doing overhaul while they waited for the last thin waft of smoke to fade into the clear blue of a Florida morning. A forest of oaks surrounded the meadow. In the center of the meadow lay in one blackened heap of rubble what remained of a small house. It had been little more than a shack even before the fire. Afterward, not even a wall remained fully standing. Threadlike tendrils of smoke oozed out of the black mass.

A pair of run-down mobile homes also occupied the clearing—one to the rear of the burned house, the other over against the edge of the little meadow. Trash barrels and other odds and ends of beer bottles and car parts lay strewn about. The place looked like a Gypsy camp, the fire cop thought, as he parked his car and sauntered over to the charred pile of smoldering rubble.

"Who lives in the trailers?" he asked a firefighter.

"Kinfolk. A whole clan lives in here. They're all either at the hospital or the morgue. Four of them were dead in the fire. We pulled 'em out. Three others had burns. The two couples from the mobile homes are in Live Oak at the hospital with the three injured."

Anderson nodded. He was a thick-barreled man who that day wore jeans, checkered short-sleeved shirt, and a blue ball cap pulled over hair rapidly turning full gray. He had been in this business more years than he sometimes liked to remember.

"So," he asked, "how many people were in the house when it went up?"

"Seven. Three got out alive."

From firefighters and deputies still on the scene, Anderson gleaned some background on the dead and injured and possible witnesses from the mobile homes.

Mabel Thompson, a 78-year-old widow, owned the house. She still took care of her two adult sons, Farrill, 45, and Roger, 40, both of whom were legally deaf and blind. Her daughter Sylvia, 50, was also blind and lived in the house. Also crammed into the house were a 17-year-old nephew, Mrs. Thompson's 57-year-old brother, and his 3-year-old son.

All had little education and even fewer skills or trades. Distressed, discontented, and in debt, the clan managed a hardscrabble living from disability checks and government welfare.

Four were dead, burned alive in the house fire. The dead were the elderly widow Mable Thompson; her two blind and deaf sons, Farrill and Roger; and her blind daughter Sylvia. Mable's brother, his 3-year-old son, and the teenager escaped. They were in serious condition with third-degree burns but were expected to survive.

The widow's third son, Ralph, and his wife lived in one mobile home, while Mrs. Thompson's remaining daughter, Rose, lived with her husband Herman Donahue in the other trailer.

"What we need to know," Suwannee County Sheriff Robert Leonard requested of fire cop Ike Anderson, "is whether the fire was accidentally or deliberately set."

Florida's Bureau of Fire and Arson Investigation had been set up as a state agency to assist small-town and rural law-enforcement agencies in investigating suspicious fires. Its agents had full law-enforcement powers, including the power of arrest and the serving of warrants. BATF simply did not have the manpower to conduct every arson investigation.

Anderson and his shovel dived into the char, even before it had cooled. Within the hour, he came across a section of concrete slab in the kitchen that lay broken in various-sized chunks, a telltale condition fire investigators recognized as spaulding. He isolated further spaulding in what was once the living room and in the bedroom. He also recovered an empty gasoline can.

Spaulding is caused by the intense heat of a liquid accelerant that is poured onto concrete and ignited. Anderson telephoned Sheriff Leonard.

"I suppose this one falls under bureau jurisdiction," he drawled. "What we have here is arson—and murder. Four homicides and three attempted homicides."

Chapter

47

Miami, Florida

Carrying an armload of stuffed file folders—mostly old unsolved arson cases—Captain Rocky McAllister brushed the papers on his cluttered desk to one side, then sank into his chair and, with a sigh, began going through the files one at a time.

He *knew* he recognized the name *Afif Yordi*. He had recognized it the first time it came up; he simply could not place it from where. From a previous case perhaps?

High property values in south Florida, inflexible zoning boards, poverty, and old buildings had made arson a thriving business in Florida. Cumulatively, the cases on McAllister's desk portrayed a world in flames—blazing towering infernos, serial arsonists and lunatics, crooked politicians, victims buried in ashes, flaring tempers and frustrated employees, lovers tossing gasoline on each other, all-but-invisible clues that must be tracked through morasses of shady characters that only a world crossroad like Miami might produce. Gritty stories, tragedies, the waging of an unwinnable war in one of the most culturally and racially diverse cities in America.

An acetone case caught his eye. This particular brain

surgeon had overlooked the stove pilot light when he sloshed acetone around his ex-girlfriend's apartment. The fumes ignited and blew him through the sliding glass doors and out into the street. The explosion dropped the inner condo wall onto an old lady bedridden next door; she died. The guy was in prison on a manslaughter conviction.

Take the case of one hotel, which was abandoned after the county zoning board refused to grant the owner permits to make structural changes. Fire burned it to the ground, spreading to the little shotgun shack next door, where it consumed two children. Their screams awakened neighbors, but by then the flames were impenetrable.

Afterward, McAllister learned that the motive behind the arson was to make room for the construction of a massive new high-rise.

There was a photo of a smiling Paddy Richardson in his file. McAllister slid his hand slowly over the case cover, as though reliving the heat and the pain of that tragic night. Richardson was a firefighter killed in the line of duty while battling a warehouse fire much like the IWDC blaze. Three other people also perished. Paddy's wife stood grief-stricken at the edge of the secure zone.

"Was it arson?" she asked McAllister.

McAllister looked away.

An edge of bitterness crept into her voice. "I would like to think Paddy was killed fighting a fire started by an act of God—not at the hand of some firebug lunatic. . . ."

As soon as the investigator came to the Sedanos Grocery file, it struck a strong chord of memory. A large tag on it read OPEN. The date of the fire was April 17, 3 years earlier. It was also a large-loss fire, over $3 million. *And* it was an acetone fire, an overt arson that destroyed Sedanos, at 9688 Southwest 24th Street, in a spectacular blaze reminiscent of the IWDC fire.

The market was spread out over half a block and employed more than 30 workers. Ex-employees, distributors, neighbors, and anyone else who conducted any form of business with the store or its chain had been questioned. McAllister thumbed to the witness list, nearly two pages filled with names. Fuhrman from the police department and BATF's Hamilton had run background checks on all witnesses and questioned most either in person or over the telephone. All current employees had been questioned face-to-face.

McAllister ran a forefinger down the list until it caught on a name.

Afif Yordi.

Excited, Rocky telephoned Hamilton, then Fuhrman. "I *told* you I knew that name."

The report listed Yordi as a "disgruntled employee."

"That alone is enough to convict him if he worked for the post office," Fuhrman growled.

Two big fires, each with a loss in the millions, each ignited with acetone—and Afif Yordi standing with one foot in each. It was more than coincidence.

Hamilton was astonished to discover in his investigation notes that *he* had personally questioned the little Pakistani. Memory quickly returned, revived by his notes. At the time, he recalled, a check on Yordi produced a clean police record with no previous arrests or convictions. He had secured a job at the market as a stock clerk 2 weeks before the fire, working in the produce section.

"In order to case the place, learn its routine and security," Fuhrman said, surmising.

Although employed only 2 weeks, Yordi became known as contentious and argumentative. He quarreled with the assistant manager over petty issues—days off, working hours, overtime. He boasted to other workers that *he* should be boss because he was smarter and knew about operating businesses. He was about to open his own import—export firm.

When Hamilton interviewed him, the little man exhibited none of the nervousness often associated with the foreign-born confronted with authority. He simply crossed his legs comfortably and smiled. Mr. Cooperation.

"I know nothing about the fire," he recited. "I truly wish I might help you gentlemen, only I was in my home and heard nothing about the fire until I was informed in the morning."

He shrugged casually when asked about problems he had had with management.

"I am not the only one who has had trouble with them. It's like that everywhere, I presume—labor and management in strife. You gentlemen should know that, really."

Nothing subsequent in the dead-end Sedanos investigation had led back to Afif Yordi.

Until then.

Chapter

48

Live Oak, Florida

The morning following the fatal house fire, investigator Ike Anderson picked up his longtime partner and friend, Fred Respress, and together they took the road 7 miles south out of Live Oak to the Gypsy meadow. Respress was close enough in style of dress and appearance to be Anderson's brother, except he favored straw Western hats over baseball caps. The two men had solved many arson cases together in Florida's northern district.

Anderson had already determined the fire to be arson; he and Respress would use the day to question witnesses and survivors. For all the value of physical and trace evidence, the best and most common evidence remained the testimony of an eyewitness.

Ralph, one of the dead woman's sons and a gaunt, unkempt man, answered Respress's knock at his trailer house door. He wore ratty jeans and no shirt. He yawned and rubbed his eyes.

"Yeah?"

The fire cops introduced themselves. "We need to ask some questions."

"I'll tell you what I can," he said. "Let me get a cup of coffee. Want one?"

Of Mabel Thompson's three sons and two daughters, only Ralph was not blind or deaf or both. He and his sister, Rose, who lived in the other mobile home with her husband, were the only siblings still alive after the previous day's predawn holocaust. He tossed dirty clothing off a couple of kitchen chairs and motioned the officers to sit. He took the sofa.

"I heard my mother's house go up, like with a big whoosh," he narrated, prompted occasionally by the investigators. "I run to the window and seen her house on fire. It was that fast. I run over there barefooted. What I seen was my teenage cousin Jody. He was the only one outside, so I knowed my mama and everybody else who lived there had to be trapped inside.

"I run in through the kitchen to try and get my mama out, but the kitchen floor was so hot it purt near burned my feet off. I just couldn't go any further. I had to go on back outside with Jody."

"Any ideas on how the fire started?" Anderson asked, omitting any reference to spaulding on the concrete floor or the empty gasoline cans he had recovered.

"Yessir, I do indeed. It had to be the gas stove in the kitchen. They've been having problems with it for a long time. The guys from the Live Oak Gas Company has been out several times, but they ain't never seemed to fix it."

Mrs. Thompson's surviving daughter Rose and her 66-year-old husband, Herman Donahue, who both lived in the other trailer, agreed with Ralph's assessment of how the fire ignited.

"It probably started from the leaky gas stove in the kitchen," Donahue asserted. "The gas company has done sent out men to fix it several times, but it still leaked."

Donahue had the wasted, busted-veins-in-the-nose appearance of an alcoholic and admitted to being one.

"My mother-in-law," he said, "always left the kitchen door open and a big pot of coffee on the stove for anybody who wanted a cup. Anybody in the family, even strangers, was always welcome to stop in for coffee any time of the day or night. I went in myself last night for a cup."

"About what time was that?" Anderson asked.

"Why, it had to be several hours before the fire—maybe a bit after midnight."

Rose Donahue felt her way to the door and followed the investigators into the yard. Donahue stood in the door, watching. Once they were out of his earshot, Mrs. Donahue whispered, "I may be near deaf and blind, but I would sure know if my husband, asleep in the bed beside me, got up in the middle of the night and went out."

Donahue—standing in the trailer doorway—appeared to be most interested in the conversation. Anderson turned his back to the alkie and shielded Rose from his view.

"Are you saying he never left the trailer?"

"He positively did not leave this mobile home all last night."

"How do *you* think the fire started?" Respress asked.

"I would guess it has to be the leaky stove."

As the fire cops drove to the hospital in Live Oak to question the night's survivors, they engaged in the familiar give-and-take of detectives in the middle of a case.

"Ralph Thompson?" Anderson asked, soliciting his partner's opinion.

"Lying," Respress responded. "He was barefooted and yet—"

"There were no burns on his feet."

"Partner, you *are* observant."

"And Herman Donahue?" Anderson continued.

"Also lying. Maybe they're all lying."

On the way to the hospital, the detectives checked the dead family's repair bills on the alleged leaking gas stove. A single service ticket on file at the Live Oak Gas Company showed the stove had been repaired in March, a year earlier.

"There have been no complaints since then," a service manager assured the investigators.

Jody the teenager was rapidly recovering from his injuries. His uncle and the uncle's 3-year-old son were more severely burned.

"I was sleeping on the floor in the living room when I heard some, like, strange noises in the kitchen," Jody said. "Like walls cracking, like something settling. I got up to see what it was. I smelled gas as I started to the kitchen. Then I seen a man walking out the back door. He was no sooner out the door than the whole entire kitchen just, like, went up in fire."

"The man?" Respress said, probing. "Did you recognize him?"

"It was dark and I only seen the back of him."

"What was he wearing?"

"Like, black pants and a black top. I thought that was kind of funny, because most people have on pajamas or something at that time of night."

"Go on," Anderson said encouragingly. "What happened after you saw the man walk out?"

"The whole kitchen was afire. I was screaming for everybody to wake up and get outside. As soon as I heard sounds of them moving around, I grabbed the telephone and yelled at the operator to get the fire department out here. I thought I had everything taken care of—so I ran out of the house myself.

"My Uncle Ralph came running up. I told him what happened and that the fire department was on the way."

"Then Ralph ran into the house to try to save his mother?" Respress said.

Jody blinked. "He didn't go in the house to try to save anybody," he countered.

"Are you sure?"

"I ought to know. He was standing right there beside me all the time, waiting for the fire department. Uncle Herman and them came running up just as the fire engines did. The firemen got my Aunt Mabel and Farrill and Roger and Sylvia out of the house, but it was already too late. They was dead from the fire. My other uncle and his little kid was alive but was in awful shape. Their clothes had caught on fire."

As the detectives prepared to leave, Anderson asked once more, "Are you certain you didn't recognize the man you saw leaving the kitchen before the fire?"

"I only seen him from the back, like I said."

Anderson paused in the Florida sunshine outside. He removed his cap and ran his fingers thoughtfully through his thinning gray hair.

"I think if we dig deeply enough here," he commented, "we'll find some kind of intrigue between the surviving members of the widow Thompson's family."

Chapter

49

In politics, fire departments are primarily a one-issue lobby, arguing repeatedly that if water sprinklers were mandated by law to be placed in *all* dwellings, then tragedies like that of the Thompson family in Live Oak and many of the 10,000 other people who burn to death annually could be avoided or at least dramatically reduced in number. *Never* had more than two people died in a single fire in which the building was equipped with an operational sprinkler system. Former fire-fighter turned journalist Dennis Smith has estimated that 8,000 lives a year might be saved by residential sprinkler laws.

Fire investigator Vance Irik, Miami Beach Fire Department, understood the frustration of pushing fire safety. Inspecting buildings, enforcing fire codes, and speaking before city commissions and other political bodies about proposed fire laws, standards, planning and development, and building codes were all part of a fire cop's job. He knew most states had guidelines *recommending* that owners of high-rise condominiums and apartment buildings have fire-safety systems—sprinklers, escape routes, fire-proof walls, and the like—installed in order to prevent a towering inferno of the type seen in the 1974 Paul Newman movie of that title.

Yet, most cities are "progress oriented." Regulations that sometimes get in the way of progress are either ignored or, when necessary, challenged in court, no matter how vocally fire-safety officers argue that omissions of fire-safety features in new buildings can lead only to tragedy. Politicians are not going to let *anything* impede progress. Conveniently countering that studies show measures other than sprinkler systems are just as effective at fire control, they often neglect to hold developers to state building guidelines. Even tenants go against fire safety, claiming their rents will increase if apartment buildings are forced to install sprinklers.

"How much is a human life worth?" big Vance Irik demands. "Apparently, not very damned much when it comes to politicians in bed with big business. We tell them what's wrong and how to prevent deaths. We tell them people are going to be trapped by fire. But nobody wants to hear about fire safety officers' and fire investigators' recommendations until it's too late."

Chapter

50

Miami Beach, Florida

David Mejia, a successful artist who enjoyed the fashionable artiste's social life of South Beach, moved to his tenth-floor apartment in the Columbine Tower to be near the action. He was a thin, sensitive-looking man who attempted to hide approaching middle age beneath youthful clothing, a ponytail, and an earring. One rainy spring night, unable to sleep at 2 A.M., he got up and stood at his window overlooking the brilliantly light-bejeweled spit of land made famous in its heyday by Jackie Gleason.

Columbine Tower was now going to seed, a bit, but Mejia cared to live nowhere else. It suited him. It was one of those buildings exempted from state guidelines on fire codes.

Mejia loved this city. He drank in a deep breath. He loved the ocean salt that seasoned the air.

He frowned. He thought he smelled smoke, something burning. He stuck his head out the window and let his gaze run down the sheer wall of the tower toward the street 100 feet below. He saw nothing unusual, not even a crack addict taking a stroll through the parking lot. He closed the window again.

He was in the kitchen draining what was left of a carton of orange juice when he heard the scream of a siren. It came down *his* street. He hurried back to the window to take a look, finding that his entire world had changed during the few minutes it took him to go to the refrigerator.

Smoke surged into the room through the window when he opened it. A faint orange glow reflected against it, as though off a campfire glimpsed at a distance through fog.

Fire!

Fighting panic, he hurried to his bedroom to snatch up and scramble into a pair of sweatpants. Heaven forbid that he run from a fire in his underwear. He hastened into the hallway to find it crammed with other half-dressed residents who were dashing about, shouting and screaming at one other. Down at the far end, smoke launched out of the stairwell, as though from a furnace. It filled the hallway, roiling and seething and making eyes burn and throats itch. A couple of men pounded on the elevator door, but it refused to open.

"We can't get down the stairs!" screeched a terror-stricken voice. "We're *trapped!*"

So great is humankind's mindless fear of its greatest enemy that fire victims have been known to panic and trample each other to death, to crowd into corners and suffocate, to blindly knock each other down stairs and elevator shafts. An announcement from a hall window temporarily defused the mounting terror.

"The fire department is here!"

The news seemed to work a miracle. Even Mejia, also on the verge of attempting something rash, composed himself and walked back to his apartment.

"Go back inside your homes," he shouted with unexpected presence. "The air will be better inside until firefighters rescue us."

You're going to burn to death, he thought, *but don't panic.*

Any sense of security he might have acquired proved fleeting once he found himself alone. Remembering having heard that damaged wiring could blow sparks and speed the spread of fire, he raced through the apartment unplugging appliances. It gave him something constructive to do.

Temperatures rose as heat radiated through the walls and floor. He wet a towel and carried it with him. The air conditioner pumped in smoke until he unplugged it. He had never felt so helpless in his life. His tongue felt dry and swollen and threatened to block his windpipe. His heart pounded against his rib cage. He was about to hyperventilate. He sat on the edge of his bed and tried to think calming thoughts.

What if the firefighters can't reach me? What if they can't break through?

He threw up his bedroom window sash and stuck his head outside into the smoke, looking for a fire escape. He had never even considered fire escapes before tonight. There were none.

Below, a traffic jam had ensued as fire trucks attempted to work down the narrow street and through the parking lot to reach the building. Firefighters and cops ran around yelling and waving their arms.

"Up here! We're up here!" Mejia shouted, but the firefighters couldn't hear him. Smoke, darkness, and the height of his window concealed him. Wreckers were hauling away parked cars to get them out of the way. *"Run over them! Push the sons of bitches out of the way!"*

He returned to sit on his bed. That didn't help. He was living the worst kind of nightmare, one from which there was no awakening. Curiosity, more than hope, drew him back to the window. Two floors below him, still eight stories up from the parking lot, a desperate battle and race against time was being waged. The drama mesmerized the frightened artist.

Flames on the eighth floor had driven a man from his apartment and onto his window ledge. He hung on the windowsill by his fingertips. His bare legs kicked over open space as though he was trying to obtain a toehold; the window belched smoke and flames flapped around the shutters. His thin screams of terror fell out of the air like broken icicles.

Firefighters worked frantically to get a hydraulic ladder started. Hard streams of water arced up through the heavy black-and-brown air. They captured the red glow of the fire and reminded Mejia, always the artist, of thick streams of shooting lava. Pumper crews dared not direct water upon the fire in the window for fear of washing the man from his precarious roost.

He was slipping. He couldn't hold on much longer. He looked up and saw Mejia. He was an older man, a little Jewish gentleman Mejia had seen around but whose name presently eluded him. He had always dressed nicely and looked most dignified. That night, he wore only a pair of striped boxers and had no dignity left.

Mejia and the doomed man gazed deep into each other's eyes. Mejia read his lips.

"Help me? Please help me?"

"What . . . ?" Mejia cried, tears streaming down his cheeks. "What can I do?"

"Help me!"

"I can't help you," Mejia whispered, his mind seared and revulsed by that acceptance and by the fear he saw in the old man's eyes.

Horrified and unable to watch the inevitable conclusion, the artist backed away from his window. He slammed it closed, erecting barriers against the unavoidable. He covered his face with both hands. They filled with sweat and tears.

FIRE COPS

The scream began loudly, trailing off as the little Jewish man's body hurtled toward earth, arms and legs windmilling as though to climb back up the smoke. Mejia* shuddered and cried out at the instant he expected the body to hit the parking lot.

---

*Two men died in the Columbine Tower blaze. David Mejia went to a city commission hearing afterward and testified that sprinklers and fire escapes installed in the building would have saved those two men's lives. Escaping death often creates fire-safety converts and crusaders.

Chapter

51

Miami, Florida

Fire cops periodically checked on the Yordi residence during the cool tropical days of late winter and early spring, waiting on Afif and his cousin Kamal Jurdi to reappear. They carefully avoided being seen by the mother and daughter Yordis. Agent Bill Hamilton wanted the mice to feel secure enough again to come out of hiding. Rumor had it that Afif and Kamal had fled to Pakistan, never to return to face questioning and possible criminal charges in the United States.

"The little turd'll be back," Detective Wil Fuhrman sourly predicted. "Life's too hard in Pakistan. If nothing else, they can claim oppressed–minority status in America and go on welfare. Besides, they've got to be thinking about that cool half-million waiting at the insurance company for them. All they have to do is wait for the heat to cool, so to speak, then return and file for it. We still can't *prove* it was *their* acetone that started the fire or that *they* did it."

"We'll prove it," McAllister vowed. "Sooner or later."

Rumors also persisted that the reason Carib Tech

had not filed an insurance claim was because Afif was dead, caught in the warehouse blaze. Kamal, the rumors insinuated, had dragged his cousin's charred body from the fire scene and deposited it in the Everglades for the alligators to consume. Fuhrman made a point of auditing the recovery of all unidentified corpses in the state. There were a considerable number of such corpses in a drug capital like Miami.

Periodically, TV news media decided to air the obligatory "remember when it happened?" story and a reporter would telephone one of the investigators.

"What progress have you made?" the reporter would ask.

"It's still under investigation."

"Are there any suspects?"

"We can only tell you we're making progress."

Inevitably, the reporters went on the air with something along the lines of "The probe of the $12 million arson fire at the International Warehouse Distributing Corporation has fallen flat. Investigators have little evidence, few leads, and apparently no suspects. In terms of loss, the fire that occurred in the early morning hours of last September third was the most destructive in recent Miami history. . . ."

In the early spring, fire detectives learned that Denise Feinweld, an emergency-department nurse at Palmetto Hospital, had had a hellish day on September 3, the day of the IWDC fire. As a result, a seriously burned patient had slipped through the cracks and escaped police scrutiny and the vigilant eye of TV, that repository of every conceivable disaster.

Denise worked until nearly midnight the previous evening, covering for a pediatrics nurse who had a hot date with a doctor. When she got home, she discovered her boyfriend had stripped the apartment bare and moved out without so much as leaving a note. She slept fitfully that night, then dragged herself out of bed for the afternoon shift, only to find her car wouldn't start. She spent what cash she had on a taxi.

"Girl, you look like you've not slept in days!" exclaimed the off-going emergency department nurse, already gathering up her things when Denise walked in to relieve her. "I've got to get home and meet my kids when they get out of school. All the usual emergency cases from this morning have been logged."

Patients were lined up, waiting without patience. The other two nurses on duty in the department were on telephones. An elderly woman with bloodshot eyes staggered up to the counter. "How much longer?" she demanded. Behind her, a bunch of other people with their own ailments demanded the same attention. On top of all this, her telephone kept ringing off the desk. Denise answered it first to escape more immediate demands.

A man identified himself as an arson investigator with the Metro–Dade Fire Department. "We need to know," he said, "if you've had anyone show up there either last night or early this morning with a fire injury."

"Hold a second."

Denise batted back tears of fatigue and frustration. She thumbed down the clipboard log on the admissions desk. Chest pains, eye injury, knife wound, unexplained bleeding . . .

"We have had no burn victims either last night or today," she told the man on the phone.

She hadn't seen the *second* page of the admissions list. There, halfway down, was the name of a man brought into the hospital shortly after dawn on September 3 suffering from second- and third-degree burns: *Afif Yordi.*

He had received emergency treatment, then left,

refusing to be admitted. He had been more dead than alive.

In the meantime, while the waiting game dragged on in Miami, fire starters continued their unrelenting drive to burn down America.

Chapter

52

Muskogee, Oklahoma

Flame-seared corpses, even when the victims can't be saved, and especially if the corpses are those of children, haunt the sleep of many firefighters who found them. Fire Marshal Norman Rogers sorted resolutely through the blackened ruins of last night's residential fire at 214 Jefferson Street. It was a disagreeable task, looking for the bodies of four children and their mother—but it came with the job of investigating suspicious fires.

The odor of char and smoke and the sickly sweet stench of burned flesh lay like a pall over the spindly skeleton of what had been a two-story single-family residence in one of Muskogee's less affluent neighborhoods. The house, a patched-up firetrap to begin with, had ultimately entombed five people, the youngest of which was 2-year-old Tiffany Marie Foster. Her tiny carbonized body, looking like a partially burned doll, lay beneath smoldering ashes on what had formerly been the living-room floor. She had apparently fallen through from her second-floor bedroom.

Rogers had the body photographed and taped off for evidence. He tried to tell himself that a dead child was nothing more than another piece of evidence, like a fingerprint or a gas can with the lid removed, but the sickness in his stomach disagreed with him.

Most of the walls had burned, leaving only a blackened framework. Firefighters extended ladders across remaining beams to provide the fire marshal and other investigators a stable platform on the second floor. Using the ladders, Rogers and Fire Captain Roger Carter located Ledavon Foster, 30, or at least what remained of her, in the master bedroom. She died with her face buried inside a box fan, as if trying to crawl into the fan to escape the violent encroachment of the flames.

The rented house had been small, with two rooms downstairs—a living room and kitchen–dining room. Upstairs were a bathroom and three small bedrooms connected by a short hallway. The master bedroom was at the rear, with a window opening onto the backyard. That was where fire cops found the mother.

The middle bedroom contained no corpses. It apparently belonged to 8-year-old Brian Burks. Fire Captain Buddy Capps found him and his two younger sisters in the front third bedroom. He speculated Brian might have bravely rushed from his own bedroom to the bedroom shared by his three sisters in an attempt to rescue them. He died with his head buried in the ashes of bedclothes next to the bed.

Nikki Lee Foster, 3, died underneath the bed. The ashes collapsed on her. Kristi Burks, 7, died on top of the bed. Little Tiffany somehow fell through to the living-room floor below.

Captain Capps looked at the misshapened little bodies and turned away. "They were trying to get away," he said, "but there was no place to go."

Muskogee Police Captain Richard Slader drove the first patrol car to respond to the fire scene at 10:33 P.M. He arrived 2 minutes after a neighbor's 911 call.

"The fire was really getting to it," he advised Norman Rogers as the investigation began with the interviewing of witnesses. "There were flames coming out all the windows. There were a couple of explosions. You could hear something zinging, like electrical wires. The house was totally involved."

A man ran toward Slader from the backyard—a skinny man with scraggly shoulder-length hair, buck naked except for an open work shirt pulled over his shoulders.

"My family's still in the house upstairs!" he cried.

Another man, later identified as neighbor John Trelling, crouched heroically near the back porch trying to cool down the upstairs window with a garden hose so he could launch a rescue attempt. The heat drove him back as fire trucks arrived with sirens screaming. Soon, fire and police equipment filled narrow Jefferson Street.

The house was constructed of wood—*old* wood. Firefighters called it a "balloon structure" because it was open all the way from the first floor through the second floor and attic to the roof with no fire stops anywhere. Flames flew freely with the flow of air. They appeared thickest upstairs in the front southeast corner.

Knowing people were trapped inside, firefighters laid pipe and hurled everything they had at the fire monster. By that point, the house was an inferno that resisted blasts of water. Blistering steam rose inside the cloud of smoke and threw back all rescue attempts. The naked man seemed to be going into shock. A firefighter asked him the same question three times: "Are you all right?"

"My wife's in the house," he finally murmured.

It took fighters over an hour to extinguish the fire and another several hours for the rubble to cool sufficiently for them to enter the smoldering rubble to search for bodies. Dawn cracked thinly over the city; the naked man from the backyard identified himself as Curtis Foster Jr., 34. Rescuers transported him to the county hospital for examination and treatment. The only survivor, he said his wife and four children had gone up in flames.

Muskogee Police Sergeant Johnny Teehee questioned Foster in the emergency department. The grieving man said he and his family had gone to bed early, at 8:01 P.M., it being a school day and workday the next morning. He said he drank "a few beers" before he went to bed and made love to his wife.

A loud noise jarred him awake.

" 'Wha' the hell!' " he had exclaimed, then jumped out of bed. "My wife hollers, 'My babies!' real loud."

Foster said he ordered his wife to escape out the bedroom window onto the roof of the back porch while he went for the children. The bedroom was filled with smoke. He heard the children screaming. He looked down the hallway and saw little Nikki on fire. He tried to get to her, he said, but the heat and smoke drove him back.

"I couldn't breathe," he mourned. "It was like superheat. . . ."

He remembered clutching his wife's hand at some point while breaking out an escape route through his upstairs bedroom window. Somehow, he lost her in the confusion. He tried to go back inside after her but couldn't because of the intense heat.

"I was yelling at the window for her to get out. I don't know how many times. I don't hear—I mean, I don't hear anything, period. There's no sound coming from the house that I can remember.

"Next thing I know, I'm on the porch roof. I ask my neighbor if my wife got out. She hadn't."

"Do you have any idea how the fire started?" Sergeant Teehee asked him.

"The only thing I can think of is electrical lines."

The unmistakable odor of gasoline hung heavy over the ruins, prompting fire cops to consider arson, not electricity, as the cause. A "normal" blaze spreads upward and outward from a central source, starting small and gradually eating out and growing larger as it consumes fuel. *This* fire gutted the house almost immediately, burning so fiercely it took high-pressure hoses an hour to kill it. That scenario generally indicates the presence of an accelerant.

Using a hydrocarbon detector (HD), Fire Marshal Rogers and his investigators soon located and identified the unmistakable residue of gasoline. Using videotape and slides of the fire and its aftermath, they constructed a burn pattern of how and where the fire started and how it progressed.

"You go from the lesser amount of damage to the most severe," Assistant Fire Marshal Robert Rhoden explained to District Attorney John David Luton. "Where you find the most severe burning, you normally find the point of origin."

The most severe damage—thus, the likely origin of the fire—occurred in the upstairs southeast bedroom where the three little girls slept. Investigators estimated some 3 to 5 gallons of gasoline had been sloshed about the house. A "trailer" of gasoline burn led from the door of each upstairs bedroom and the bathroom, down the stairway to the living room and kitchen–dining room. Curtis Foster's work jeans lay, partly consumed by fire, in front of the upstairs bathroom sink.

The house had been so soaked in gasoline that it literally erupted like a volcano once it was ignited. *Someone* wanted to make damned sure nothing was left.

"Something had to keep Ledavon from her children," insisted the dead woman's tearful aunt. "She was a strong woman. She would have got out of that house and got her kids out if she was able to move. I saw her jump right off the top of a two-story barn once. She would have smashed through a second-story window without even thinking about it."

Chapter

53

Live Oak, Florida

Investigator Ike Anderson's blind and deaf victims likewise had little chance of escaping. Their house also erupted like a volcano once spilled gasoline was ignited. In this fire too, *someone* had wanted to make damned sure nothing was left.

But why? That same old question that plagued each arson case—*Cui bono?* (Who benefits?)—troubled Ike Anderson and Fred Respress. They delved deeply into the family's affairs, suspecting intrigue. They requestioned the 17-year-old nephew who, along with his uncle and his uncle's 3-year-old son, survived the blaze.

"I have a gut feeling he knows a lot more than he's told us," Anderson remarked.

Pressed by the fire detectives, the youth, reluctantly at first, then more freely with each passing word, shed some light onto existing tensions in the little glade. Most of the dissension, it seemed, orbited around Herman Donahue, the boy's uncle by marriage, married to Mabel Thompson's only surviving daughter.

"Uncle Herman is the black sheep of the family," the boy explained. "Everybody is real scared of him, especially my other uncle."

"Why so?" Respress prompted.

"He's low-down mean. He's been in and out of prison a number of times. He only got paroled a week ago after doing a year for shooting a woman over in Live Oak."

"Tell us about it," Anderson requested.

At the time, temporarily separated from Rose and the Thompson clan, Donahue lived alone in his mobile home in Live Oak. One night a year earlier, the teenager said, "He had a woman there with him and they were polishing off six-packs of beer. Uncle Herman was afraid they'd run out, so he took off to buy more beer. When he got back, the woman had finished off all the beer left in the refrigerator. So he shot her."

Anderson's brow arched. "Just like that? For drinking the last of the beer?"

"Yep."

The woman was semicomatose not only from her gunshot wound but also from having consumed prodigious quantities of beer. Donahue dragged her into the bedroom and put her on the bed. He returned to his drinking in the kitchen.

A short time later, he heard his pickup truck start up. He ran to the door in time to see his taillights disappearing out of the drive.

"He panicked, called the sheriff's department, and reported that someone had just stolen his truck. Police stopped the truck almost immediately and found Uncle Herman's woman friend at the wheel."

She told officers she had climbed out Donahue's bedroom window and stole the truck in order to escape. Patrolmen returned to the trailer and told Donahue they had received a report of a woman having been shot. They wanted to see her.

"She's in the back bedroom sleeping," Donahue replied. "She's okay."

"We'd like to see her for ourselves."

The teenage nephew grinned. "Uncle Herman almost

passed out when he took them back there and she wasn't on the bed. He got a year in prison for shooting her. Like I said, he got out only a week ago and moved his mobile home into the clearing behind Aunt Mabel's house."

Anderson continued the questioning. "You said your uncle Ralph, your blood uncle, was scared of Herman."

"Yep. When Uncle Herman moved his trailer in last week, Uncle Ralph took a string and run it around his trailer. Every night he tied the end of the string to his toe so it would jerk his toe and wake him up if Uncle Herman tried to sneak up on him."

Anderson and Respress looked at each other, suppressing laughter at the image.

"Like a booby trap?" Anderson said.

"Yeah."

"Why was Ralph so afraid of Herman?"

"It didn't take much to make Uncle Herman shoot. Like when he shot that woman."

Uncle Ralph blew up when the detectives confronted him with his nephew's statement.

"You can't believe a damned thing that kid tells you," he shouted. "He's a lying little . . . He'll tell you anything you want to hear. I don't know why you're even talking to him. He's a juvenile to begin with."

Shooting the woman over his beer was not Herman Donahue's first brush with the law. He started his way through the prison system when he was 18, convicted of a nonfatal shooting in Georgia. Since then, he had served three other sentences for aggravated battery. But having a police rap sheet four pages long fell short of proof that he'd set the fire being investigated.

It would seem that were Donahue to torch anything, it would be Ralph's trailer, not the old lady's house. How had burning Mabel Thompson's home benefitted him? She had been good to him, allowing him to live on her property. Nothing about her death or the deaths of the other victims provided him with any apparent gain.

Donahue's name was not in Mabel Thompson's will. She owned little of value once the house was gone—and, besides, the entire clan was being supported by government checks received by Mabel and her now-dead sons and daughter.

The remaining Thompsons and Herman Donahue were having to tighten their belts, what with the major wage earners now gone. Why, they might even have to find *work.*

Some of these questions were answered when investigator Respress made a call on a friend who happened to know Ralph Thompson quite well. The friend affirmed the teenage nephew's assertion that Uncle Ralph was indeed afraid of Herman Donahue. Furthermore, one of the reasons Ralph was afraid of him was because he believed Donahue burned out Mabel and her blind and deaf children.

"I know there was a lot of animosity between Herman Donahue and Ralph Thompson," the friend explained. "Once Herman got out of prison last week and moved his trailer onto the clearing, it didn't take him 24 hours to discover Ralph had a good thing going." Apparently, Ralph had taken charge of the family's finances, collecting and distributing all the government checks being issued to the various members of the family. The friend suspected Ralph was afraid her men would take over his collection duties and turn it into what the friend termed "a good scam."

"Got the picture," Respress said. "Go on."

"Ralph accused Donahue of setting the fire. Donahue got mad and went out and bought a pistol. He pointed the gun at Ralph and told him he'd better keep such thoughts to himself."

"And, apparently," said Respress dryly, "that's what the surviving Thompsons have been doing—keeping such thoughts to themselves."

Chapter

54

Muskogee, Oklahoma

The single survivor of the holocaust that claimed his wife and four children grew increasingly distressed as Police Sergeant Johnny Teehee and Fire Marshal Norman Rogers questioned him about the tragedy.

"Could someone with a grudge have broken into your house and set it afire while you slept?" they asked Curtis Foster. The medical examiner had already reported autopsy findings: none of the five victims bore head injuries or other trauma sustained before the fire; they were alive and conscious when the fire began.

"We kept the doors locked," Foster said, then suggested that a labor union dispute at the tire factory where he worked might have been behind it. "To get even," he added.

Foster was a scab, a strikebreaker, who hired on with other nonunion workers when the local union walked out on strike at the tire factory. Some of the strikebreakers had been harassed and threatened. One woman reported the window of her parked van busted out.

"It was because I crossed the picket line," she surmised.

Another scab received anonymous threatening phone

calls. "I'll burn you out if you cross the picket line again," a man snarled.

Yet, by the day after the fire, Sergeant Teehee was opining to Fire Marshal Rogers, "I don't believe the fire is relevant to the tire company. We have no real indication that someone from the company did this."

The fire was arson, no question of that. Fire cops concentrated on witnesses in hopes of forming a motive for the blaze. Finding the motive produces a suspect at least 90% of the time.

"They were my babies!" Curtis Foster cried angrily. "I'm sorry 'cause I didn't save them."

"They seemed like such a nice family," a neighbor said. "They were always saying hi."

"He would do anything to help people," another asserted. "He showed me pictures of those children and talked about them. He adores his children. I know he did not set fire to that house and burn up those children and his wife. There's no way he did it."

Investigators refused to let emotion or incredulity deter them from following facts to wherever they led. They scrounged into Foster's background, hoping to shed some illumination into the man's psyche. Fire starters, Rogers believed from his long experience as an arson detective, were of a particular type. They were somehow *different* from ordinary criminals. Fire was almost integral to their personalities.

Gradually, information accumulated on the hapless Foster family. Theirs was a tale outlandish enough to have landed man and wife on the front pages of the tabloids.

To begin with, Curtis Foster was an ex-convict with convictions for forgery, theft, perjury, felonious possession of firearms, and other crimes. He was also a documented abuser of alcohol, drugs, and women. So much for character.

Prior to migrating to Muskogee, the family resided in the small Arkansas town of Bativa. There, Foster was married to a woman named Sharon, who was his second wife. Ledavon, who had died in the fire, had been married to a Bativan man named Chuck Burks. Foster and his wife Sharon were neighbors and friends to Chuck and Ledavon Burks. The two couples were such close friends that they switched bed partners in a kind of swinging double affair. Sharon and Ledavon each gave birth to a baby whose father was the other woman's husband. You almost needed a scorecard to keep up.

Brian and Kristi Burks were children from Ledavon Foster's marriage to Chuck Burks. The two younger girls were biologically Curtis Foster's.

Both marriages inevitably crumbled. Curtis Foster got together with Ledavon. Although he eventually married her, he continued to rendezvous with his first wife, Sharon. On at least one occasion, he left Ledavon behind while he took his ex-wife on a pilgrimage to that great Southern shrine—Elvis's Graceland. One acquaintance caustically observed that violence and wife abuse became as common in the Foster family as fleas and crooked politicians in Little Rock.

A cousin of Ledavon's informed detectives of one violent episode that occurred before the Fosters left Arkansas. The cousin lived next door.

"I was gone to church," she said. "My husband heard Ledavon's screams. Curtis had broke her arm in two, pulled it down over her shoulder. My husband took her to the hospital. We begged her to leave him then, but she said she had to try awhile longer. She was crazy in love with him—and now you see what it got her."

On another occasion, Curtis threatened to actually kill his wife. He was on his way home with a gun when police arrested him.

"He's still out on bond and awaiting trial on that," the cousin said.

In Arkansas, Ledavon worked an assembly line for a factory in nearby Harrison. Fire Marshal Rogers and

Sergeant Teehee rooted out several witnesses from the factory who recollected that the normally outgoing young woman became quiet and withdrawn during the last 2 years of her life in Arkansas.

"She came in bruised a lot—black eye, broken hand, some sort of injury," said one fellow worker. "This happened at least once a month."

Ledavon began discussing divorce. "She asked me if I knew where she could go get help and I tried to guide her in the right direction," a friend revealed. "She was wanting to get a divorce, but she had to do it without him knowing it."

The frightened wife consulted an Arkansas legal-aid society. The executive director there told fire detectives how Ledavon came in three separate times over a 1-year period. She didn't have money enough to file the first time. She failed to carry through on the second effort. Legal aides refused to accept her as a client the third time because she vacillated on her previous visits.

This pattern of abused and abuser was one all too familiar to law-enforcement officers.

Ledavon's cousin proposed that the reason Curtis Foster moved his family out of Arkansas was in order to isolate his abused wife from her family. "He wanted to beat her, and he thought if he got her away, he could do what he wanted to do. He threatened her several times with a gun, told her he'd blow her head off. I just didn't think he'd go this far. I didn't think he would set his house afire with his own kids in it."

About 3 weeks before the fatal fire, Ledavon returned to Arkansas with the children for a visit to her family. Seven-year-old Kristi Burks wailed plaintively before they returned to Muskogee, "We won't see you no more. Daddy said we'd never see you again—we'd never be in Arkansas again."

It was a prediction that came true.

One further revelation from Arkansas confirmed Norman Rogers's conviction not only that fire starters are different, but also that such propensities develop over years. No person suddenly goes out and sets a neighbor's house afire without working up to it.

Another neighbor from Bativa hesitated, reluctant to tell everything out of fear for her own safety, finally recalled for the fire cops a summer's day less than a year earlier. Going to visit Ledavon, she found Curtis standing in the doorway looking furious while Ledavon cringed on the sofa inside. Clearly they had been fighting.

"Things had been scattered around, dumped out," she said. "I smelled gasoline. . . . Ledavon said the dummy had strung gas around the house. She had kicked the gas can off the porch into a pile of weeds. She was scared to death her husband was going to burn the house down."

Fire was one of the most hideous deaths of all. Fire Marshal Rogers suspected the man had grown up with a fascination for fire, had probably been a kid setting fire to neighbors' trash and vacant lots. That was part of a fire starter's nature and background—along with a history of abusing weaker people.

Putting together an arson-murder case was a 1,000-piece puzzle, solved by finding one piece at a time and applying it to the board. The Arkansas material was background—clouds and mountains of the puzzle, if you like. Witnesses in Muskogee who knew the Fosters in that city or who had come running to the scene of the fire supplied pieces for the central theme. The puzzle was turning into an ugly picture.

A nurse at the county hospital emergency department remarked that Curtis Foster was admitted with a rather unusual odor clinging to his hair—that of gasoline. She noted he appeared especially calm, in control, considering the disaster that had just befallen his family. Sergeant Teehee himself remarked, "Foster *miraculously* comes out of this without any injuries while his wife and children are burning up inside the house. Whatever rescue attempts you make are bound to get you some type of injury."

"Unless," Rogers supplied, "you made no rescue attempts at all."

The thought seemed too horrible to even contemplate—a father setting fire to his family.

John Trelling, the man who fought the blaze with a garden hose, said, "When I looked around and noticed the fire, I saw flames shooting out the top of the house . . . and coming out of the upstairs windows and over the roof."

He sprinted across the street, kicked out the dining-room window, and yelled inside to see if anyone was trapped. No response.

Suddenly, Curtis Foster appeared, naked. "Help me! Help me!" he pleaded. "My kids are in there!"

Trelling stripped off his own shirt and gave it to Foster. It was he, *not Foster,* who then climbed to the back-porch roof and tried to enter the upstairs window. Flames forced him back and down. He resorted to fighting the fire with a garden hose until firefighters arrived.

"I was trying to see if there was any way to get into the house in front," another neighbor told fire cops. "There really wasn't. You could hear the kids inside, and they were screaming. It's a horrible sound. It's just bloodcurdling. . . . Their father wasn't making much of an effort to get back into the house."

. . . Wasn't making much of an effort . . . that statement stuck with the fire detectives. Most fathers, Tee-hee said, would have attempted to charge into the fires of hell in trying to save their children.

Three final pieces of the puzzle completed the sordid picture.

First: a search of Foster's pickup truck turned up a receipt dated a few hours before the fire for a $4 purchase of gasoline—in a container.

Second: Rogers learned Ledavon had again discussed divorcing Curtis, only 2 days before she burned to death, prompted by Curtis's having gone off again with ex-wife Sharon.

"She was just tired of him leaving and she didn't know where he was," explained a Muskogee friend. "She wanted me to help her file for divorce. She wanted to get it done and have everything prefiled, so that her husband couldn't find out. She was afraid. She said her husband told her if she even tried to leave him or divorce him, he would kill her and the children."

Two days later, they were all dead in a scene of smoke and carnage.

Third: a surprise witness, still another Muskogee neighbor, turned up. A young woman wiped tears from her eyes as she remembered a terrifying scream that shred the night air moments before the Foster home erupted. A heart-rending plea followed the scream.

"Please don't throw the gas."

"It sounded like Ledavon screaming. I ran to the window. . . . It . . . the fire was already up high, high . . . red fire, blazing fire. . . ."*

---

*Curtis Foster Jr. was convicted of first-degree arson and five counts of first-degree murder—and sentenced to life imprisonment. "If he had lined up his wife and children and shot them," an arson investigator was overheard commenting, *"that* would have been cruel and unusual and have gotten him the death penalty. But if he burns them to death . . . ? That's *not* cruel and unusual?"

Chapter

55

Nearly 7 months had passed since the IWDC arson. Files on the IWDC case, each about 3 inches thick, occupied the desks of Bill Hamilton, Rocky McAllister, and Wil Fuhrman. They contained witness interviews, insurance documentation, bills of lading, customs statements. The case remained a puzzle in which everything had been figured out with the exception of two pieces.

Those two pieces were the missing suspects—Afif Yordi and Kamal Jurdi.

Firefighters in the nineteenth century were territorial and guarded their territory jealously. Bitter competitions often existed between city fire stations. When an alarm sounded, one firefighter was sent running ahead with a barrel while the others got the horses and equipment ready. When he reached the fire, he slipped the barrel over the nearest fire hydrant. The first crew to gain control of the water hydrant had command of fighting the fire. The "barrel man" physically fought off other crews. It was a rough way to do business; it often resulted in brawls while the flames raged.

Competitions between stations still exist, but they

aren't quite so physical anymore. Captain Rocky McAllister recalled his firefighting days: jumping on top of a hose and charging with it in a crouch at the red glow because another crew was on the way and you couldn't let *them* put out the fire. Crawling into flames on his stomach, dragging that monstrous snake of a hose that weighed 90 pounds per 50 feet when it was *dry* and not charged with water. Into dense smoke that shrank vision to 2 inches in front of his nose. Pushing, crawling toward a dim glow in the background. Choking, cursing, shouting, rolling over on the hot floor and opening the nozzle and letting the enemy have it, like a machine-gun crew. A whole big room aflame, but that 2½-incher put it out in 20 seconds—and you put it out before the other crew even arrived.

McAllister had stopped going into burning buildings, at least on a regular basis. He missed it, sometimes thought of going back to it. The sense of personal confrontation, of competition, had never left his nature. Each blaze had been a personal affront when he was a firefighter; it had to be fought and extinguished. It couldn't be left burning.

He felt the same way now that he was a fire investigator. Each case is a personal affront. It can't be left burning.

On March 29, BATF agent Bill Hamilton rocked back at his desk and smiled at a framed photo on the wall of himself and his son winning a fishing tournament. The IWDC case had dragged on so long he could hardly recall if the photo was snapped before or after the fire. The rest of a summer, an entire fall and winter, and even spring had passed since he last stood in the ruins of the warehouse. The warehouse, in fact, had been razed and another was under construction in its place.

Investigations as often as not ended rather anticlimactically. This one, however, seemed to go on and on.

If Yordi and Jurdi were smart, they would *never* return to the United States.

Hamilton's phone rang. He answered it. A voice said without preamble, "Your boy is back in town with his family."

It caught Hamilton off guard.

"Bill, did you hear me?" It was the voice of an informant Hamilton had cultivated in Yordi's neighborhood. He had instructions to call the instant he spotted Afif Yordi back at his mother's house. "Afif Yordi is in town. He's here in Miami."

Whoever said criminals were smart?

"He's *not dead?*" Hamilton exclaimed.

"Not unless that was his ghost I saw."

Hamilton hung up and sat a moment to collect his thoughts. Then he telephoned McAllister and Fuhrman.

Chapter

56

Live Oak, Florida

Life for the two disparate couples in the mobile homes continued in its humdrum way in the little glade south of Live Oak, unchanged except for the mound of blackened ruins that had claimed the lives of four members of the clan. Fire cops Ike Anderson and Fred Respress had run hard against the immutable wall of family silence and bounced back to become distant observers. They made little progress in the investigation as long as the survivors refused to talk.

One month after the fatal fire, Herman Donahue was arrested for violation of probation. He failed to notify his parole officer of having moved out of Live Oak. It was as a result of this arrest that the aging ex-convict found himself thrown into a cell with a convicted burglar awaiting final sentencing. No matter how often "jailhouse confessions" to other inmates occur and are used as evidence, jailbirds can't seem to keep their mouths shut. They boast, brag, crow, and lament crimes to cellmates during long hours of confinement that they wouldn't even hint at on the outside.

State Attorney Jerry Blair received a misspelled, sloppy piece of handwriting from the Okaloosa Correctional Center in Crestview. The author was a burglar named Clyde Snipes, who alluded to a possible reduction in his sentence for information he could supply. A *murderer*, he wrote, had confessed his crimes to him while they were celled together.

The murderer's name was Herman Donahue.

Blair forwarded the letter to Ike Anderson.

"Herman told me he started the fire at the Thompson house," Snipes confided to Anderson and Respress once the two detectives snatched him out of jail for interrogation. A polygraph test verified he told the truth. "He said he hadn't intended to hurt anyone. The way he figured it, he decided to get the Thompsons to move out of the house they'd been living in for most of their lives and move into his mobile home with him. That way they'd be dependent on him. Once he had them there, *he*, not his brother-in-law, would be the one to collect and handle their government checks.

"He thought the best way to get them to move out of their old house and into his was to burn down their house. He didn't intend for anyone to get hurt in it. No one would have either, except the old lady made him mad. He went over for coffee and ran into the old woman just as she stripped to take a bath. She ordered him to get out of the house."

Donahue's well-known temper, fueled by a dozen or so beers, finally got the upper hand just before dawn of April 25. Brooding over Mabel Thompson's perceived insult of having kicked him out of her house, he stormed over with a can of gasoline, poured it all over her kitchen floor, lit a match, and ran back to his trailer to await the inevitable results. He never expected the fire to engulf the house so rapidly; he thought the Thompsons would escape, that he might even turn out to be a hero by taking them all in and soothing them afterward.

Instead, four of them died.

Once the family armor was chinked and Herman

Donahue was securely in jail where he could cause no more harm, Mrs. Thompson's teenage nephew recalled details about that fateful night he earlier failed to divulge. Asked if he recognized the dark form fleeing the kitchen moments before the fire, he hesitated before nodding. The man, he said, had spoken to him.

"If you tell anyone," the ominous intruder warned, "you're next."

"Did you recognize the voice?" fire cops asked.

"It kind of sounded like Uncle Herman Donahue.* I didn't think it was him at the time everything was happening. But, afterwards, I got to thinking about it and realized the voice was his."

---

*Herman Donahue, at 67, was subsequently convicted of four counts of manslaughter and three counts of attempted murder, burglary, and arson. He was sentenced to 30 years on each of the manslaughter convictions, 50 years on each of the attempted murders, 30 years on arson, and 15 years on burglary.

Chapter

57

Miami, Florida

Bill Hamilton was surprised that not a single scar appeared on Afif Yordi's face when he summoned the Pakistani to his office for questioning in the IWDC fire. Even his expressive hands remained thin and unscarred—no missing digits. His fine tan features with their remarkable ability to express candor and openness bore no discolored patches of skin, nor were his small-shaped ears unusually reconstructed or altered. Maybe Nurse Feinweld at Palmetto Hospital had been mistaken about it being *him* who, "more dead than alive," sought emergency treatment and then refused to be admitted. Certainly *this* man had not been in a fire.

Sitting in his chair easily in BATF's interrogation room, Yordi appeared as serene and unruffled as a monk in meditation. He smiled and widened his eyes in disbelief that he could be a suspect in a crime.

"I'm so sorry it took so long to see you," he apologized with an air of condescension that deeply annoyed Wil Fuhrman. "Had I known it was urgent, I would have returned sooner to Miami. But I have been away on business and I was not in touch with my family."

"You've been out of touch with your family for *seven months?*" Fuhrman roared.

Nothing cracked Yordi's shell. "Traveling, you understand. Oh, I sent postcards but was never in one place long enough for a response. The import–export business is awfully competitive. It's terribly hard on a family, which explains perhaps why I have not taken a wife."

"Okay. Let's start this way," Hamilton interrupted, striving for voice neutrality. "Where were you the night of the warehouse fire?"

Yordi had a bothersome quirk of repeating each question. "Where was I? What date was that?"

Fuhrman sighed and told him.

"September 3? I can't really say. Is it important that I know? It was a day or so after the fire before I found out about it. I was probably busy around town and didn't see the news or anything, so I really can't be certain about the date. I was probably home in bed at that late hour. It has been quite some time since the fire and I can't remember. I have even been too busy to file insurance claims for our losses."

The interrogation continued at a plodding pace, controlled by Yordi's deliberate repetitions and glib manner of answering without revealing anything. The criminal mind delighted as much in defeating authority and getting away with a crime as it did in committing the crime.

"Where did I go after the fire? I was very busy around town for a couple of days, then I left on a normal business trip to South America; from there, to Asia. It's all part of the business, trying to make a legitimate profit by connecting buyers here with manufacturers all over the world. . . .

"Hospital? I was never admitted to a hospital. As you see, I certainly have no burns. . . .

"Acetone and canisters? It's only part of normal business. We use acetone for a number of things, depending upon what we have imported—fats and the like. It's possible acetone is still in the possession of Carib Tech somewhere, in another storage facility. I've been out of the country for so long. . . .

"Why did I return? That should be obvious. I have my family, my business. . . ."

Apparently, mother and daughter Yordi, thinking everything had blown over once they deferred filing an insurance claim, had summoned their prodigal men home. But Yordi was not nearly as smart as he thought he was. Fire cops had no intention of permitting him to escape on a thin web of subterfuge, not after so long.

Hamilton suddenly slid his chair back. Yordi flinched. Hamilton smiled slyly as he rose to his feet.

"We'll be talking again, Mr. Yordi," he said. "You can count on it."

Investigators felt cousin Kamal Jurdi to be the weak link in the fire crime chain. The getaway driver, the inside man, the fence, the contact, the *accomplice*—he was always the weak link, there being no honor among criminals. Whereas Afif Yordi appeared devoid of any sense of guilt or responsibility for what he had done, Jurdi came across as tense and hangdog guilty. Hamilton thought he knew how to get to him. He sat down in the interrogation room and smiled at the nervous little man. The previous 7 months had been hard on him. He reminded the fire cop of Raskolnikov in Dostoyevsky's *Crime and Punishment.*

"We know certain things about this fire and can prove certain facts," the agent began. "Your cousin Afif actually set the fire, but you helped him by driving him to the warehouse. A police officer stopped you nearby, remember? The two of you *will* be charged with arson with intent to defraud the insurance company."

He paused deliberately. Jurdi sighed wearily, as though expressing his desire to have it all over with.

Hamilton continued, encouraged. "Your Aunt Nayat

and cousin Najua are also implicated. They must also be considered suspects, and as such, their immigration status is at risk. They *may* be deported."

Jurdi glanced up sharply. Hamilton continued to play him. Jurdi obviously held a great deal of affection for his aunt.

"We do, however, have some leeway when it comes to Immigration," the detective said, carefully avoiding making promises outside his jurisdiction. "You may be able to help them."

Jurdi glanced around the room, finding nothing for his eyes to settle on. He sighed again. "You can help them remain in the United States?" he asked.

"I can't promise anything. But if they *weren't* involved . . ."

Jurdi clasped his hands, worked his fingers. He straightened in his chair. He looked at Hamilton, at Fuhrman. Hamilton casually crossed his legs and tapped his pencil idly on the desk. *Hey,* the gesture said, *it doesn't make a damned bit of difference to me one way or the other.*

"Kamal," he said presently. "Kamal, tell me what happened."

And Kamal did. It's strange how criminals unidentified and at large often assume the characteristics of supercriminals, bigger than life in their deeds and cunning. Cornered, however, they return to their original shapes—common little people with shrunken, greedy souls. Detectives are often disappointed with the anticlimax of a big case.

Hamilton felt both disappointment in the nondramatic conclusion to the case and elation that he along with Fuhrman and McAllister had finally solved it.

The crime had been planned strictly for profit, Kamal confirmed. It was a simple enough scheme—inflate the value of the imported goods, burn them, and make a claim to the insurance company for the puffed-up value. It seemed foolproof.

The conspirators readily obtained 1,250 gallons of acetone, in large containers, which they broke down into more portable units of 5 gallons each in the Yordi garage. Use of the CanChem containers, although initially difficult to trace, had been the arsonists' first major mistake. They led investigators to Carib Tech.

"Why did you order them when you could have obtained unmarked jugs locally?" Fuhrman asked Jurdi.

"I don't know. I think Afif was trying to show how smart he was."

Unaware of surveillance by DEA agents, Jurdi and Yordi bundled the CanChem jugs full of acetone into two huge crates. Jurdi delivered them as a routine shipment for storage at the IWDC warehouse on September 2, before the fire that night. A passenger accompanied the shipment. Afif Yordi, the fire starter, was hidden *inside* the crates with the acetone.

So *that* was how the arsonist gained entry. Fuhrman shook his head; he should have guessed it himself.

"It worked for him twice before," Jurdi explained.

"Twice?"

Fire detectives knew about the Sedanos Market fire. Afif, Jurdi said, hid himself inside the market until after closing time, then ventured out to pour acetone or gasoline——he didn't know which——around and set the fire.

The second arson occurred 4 months later, on August 16, when Yordi accepted a contract to burn down Far East Suppliers, Inc. The owner paid Afif to torch the building to destroy records sought by U.S. Customs. Afif once again secreted himself inside the business to carry out his nefarious task.

In addition to Yordi and the acetone, inside one of the crates delivered by Jurdi to IWDC were a hot plate to be used as a timer and a walkie-talkie by which Afif would notify Jurdi's cruising van that he was ready to be picked up. Yordi, however, misunderstood some of acetone's quirks—namely, the volatility of its fumes.

Something ignited them prematurely, before Yordi could complete his job and escape. Perhaps it was a pilot light in the little coffee area, a faulty refrigerator sparking on and off, an automatic electrical switch being toggled, a frayed electric cord, even a walkie-talkie being keyed. . . .

"Afif was blown out through the door," Kamal said.

The violence of the explosion shocked Kamal, who was cruising nearby in the van. He was supposed to pick up his cousin *before* the fire started so they could be far away, establishing an alibi by the time firefighters arrived.

Alarmed, Kamal sped away in the van, thinking his cousin was surely killed.

Only—Afif lived. He regained consciousness and hobbled away into the night, causing his mother, sister, and cousin to go into near heart arrest when he staggered home at dawn. His clothing hung in flame-seared tatters. Charred skin dribbled in blackened strips from his cheeks. His nose and ears resembled chips of charcoal. Only sheer luck prevented blindness.

The Yordis loaded their injured family member into a vehicle and sped him to Palmetto Hospital for emergency treatment. It was that afternoon that Nurse Feinweld, preoccupied with personal problems, failed to notice Afif Yordi's name on the second page of the admissions list when Rocky McAllister telephoned. Yordi slipped through the cracks.

Two days later, Yordi and his cousin fled the United States, Kamal taking refuge in Asia, Yordi seeking a plastic surgeon in Latin America to reconstruct his damaged face.

"It was incredible when I saw him again," Kamal said. "It was like nothing had happened to him at all. He was as good as new."

Doctors had indeed accomplished miracles.

After Jurdi's confession, Hamilton leaned his wiry frame wearily against the doorjamb outside the room. Fuhrman grinned at him.

"Call McAllister," the agent said. "He'll want to be in on this. Let's bring in Afif Yordi. This baby is *closed*."*

---

*Afif Yordi was convicted of arson in each of three cases—Far East Suppliers, Sedanos Market, and IWDC—and sentenced to 32 years in prison, the longest sentence ever dealt an arsonist in Dade County not involving death. Kamal Jurdi testified against him and received a reduced sentence of 7 months in jail.

Afterword

It was a scene of near idyllic beauty: a 12-year-old boy pumping his bicycle along a gravel county road in rural northern California, fields of golden wheat lining either side of the road. A pickup truck passed the boy, honking its horn in friendly greeting.

In the forest in the near distance, beyond the grain fields, billows of smoke hung in the late-summer sky. A police patrol car and an unmarked sedan driven by a county arson investigator, a fire cop, kicked up rooster tails of dust as they descended upon the juvenile bicyclist.

The boy stopped. Expressions of curiosity and excitement and fright warred across his little boy's smooth face. He let his bicycle fall to the road as the cars stopped. Two uniformed men stepped out onto the road.

"Son," said the arson investigator, "we have some questions we need to ask you."

Fires had plagued the summer—arson. Thousands of acres of timberland had been burned, along with four houses. A baby died in one of the houses.

The boy burst into tears. "You think I did it, don't you? Well, *don't you?*"

273

Printed in the United States
By Bookmasters